RABBINIC-LAY RELATIONS

IN

JEWISH LAW

STUDIES IN PROGRESSIVE HALAKHAH, VOLUME II

Also in this Series

Walter Jacob and Moshe Zemer (ed.) DYNAMIC JEWISH LAW
Progressive Halakhah - Essence and Application

RABBINIC - LAY RELATIONS

IN

JEWISH LAW

Edited by
Walter Jacob and Moshe Zemer

Freehof Institute of Progressive Halakhah
Tel Aviv and Pittsburgh
Rodef Shalom Press
1993

Published by the Rodef Shalom Press
4905 Fifth Avenue
Pittsburgh, PA 15213
U.S.A.

4 Rehov Levitan
69204 Tel Aviv
Israel

4905 5th Avenue
Pittsburgh, PA 15213
U.S.A.

Library of Congress Catalog Card Number 93-083436

Jacob, Walter 1930-

Zemer, Moshe 1932-

ISBN 0-929699-04-1

This volume is dedicated

to our parents

Sarah Zager

Sam C. Zager   ז״ל

Rabbi Ernest I. Jacob   ז״ל

Annette F. Jacob   ז״ל

Table of Contents

PREFACE

We wish to express special gratitude to our colleagues, Bernard M. Zlotowitz and Susan Rheins, for their invaluable assistance with the copy-editing of this volume. We are also grateful to Joni Cohen Zlotowitz, and Maud Prince for their devotion to the typescript, to Robert Goldman for his efforts in typesetting the manuscript and to Barbara Baley for her continuous help.

This volume and its predecessor would not have been possible without the generous gifts of Admiral Joshua Goldberg. We are grateful and wish him well.

INTRODUCTION

What is the essence of a rabbi? Maimonides declared:

"There is no honor greater than the honor of a rabbi and no awe greater than that of a rabbi. The sages tell us: Let the honor of your rabbi be as the honor of God and the fear of your rabbi like the fear of Heaven - therefore they proclaimed: Contradicting your rabbi is like contradicting the Divine Presence... a controversy with your rabbi is like a controversy with the Divine Presence...resenting your rabbi is like resenting the Divine Presence." (Laws of Talmud Torah 5:1)

This Maimonidean hyperbole has been translated into modern terms with great expectations of the rabbi as preacher, teacher, scholar, officiant, counselor, community leader, etc. The authority of the Jewish spiritual leader which has always been derived from scholarship or charisma, is a key to the mastery of these many tasks.

The relationship of a rabbi and congregant is often pregnant with an ambivalent admixture of mutual love, respect, and even awe, on the one hand, and, on the other, jealousy, competition, power struggle and perhaps a dash of Oedipus/Electra thrown in.

This volume, *Rabbinic-Lay Relations in Jewish Law*, demonstrates that such ambivalence is not a product of our time alone. As we look through these pages we are convinced, with *Kohelet*, that in spite of the upheavals of the generations "there is nothing new under the sun"; or as the French so aptly put it: "*plus cà change, plus c'est la même chose*" (the more it changes, the more it's the same thing.)

Yet a closer look at the seven essays of this book reveals a different view of the rabbinic-lay relationship. Rabbinic authority may derive from scholarship of spiritual charisma, but without these qualities, a community crisis may result. Part of the relationship of the laity with rabbis is the *kavod*, the honor and respect afforded the spiritual leader. Must the rabbi earn this respect or should it be granted to him/her as the representative of Torah? The professionalization of the rabbinate heightened the tension between studying and teaching Torah for the sake of Heaven and the need to make a living.

Rabbis throughout the ages were called upon to respond with sensitivity to the ethical imperatives of those suffering from the undue "tyranny" of the *halakhah*. Many of the great sages resolved the problems of these unfortunates through *halakhic* innovation, thereby assuaging their anguish. Rabbinic arbitration, less known that rabbinic courts and judgement, may serve as a model when compromise is required and a rabbi's Torah verdict may not be authorative. Rabbis and lay people sharing authority and power in the congregation is a time tried phenomenon.

These are among the issues presented in this book. Of course there are vast differences between Jewish leadership of the past and today, yet many of the principles of interaction between rabbi and community revealed in this tome are still valid today. To use the language of the philosophers, the essence of the rabbinate, its intrinsic nature and true substances will be found in all of the above and yet will be more than the sum of these many categories. Hopefully, this book will contribute to the understanding of the Rabbinic-lay relationships.

This is the second publication of our Freehof Institute of Progressive Halakhah. It is based on a colloquium held at the 1991 CCAR Conference in Fort Lauderdale, Florida. It follows our first volume, *Dynamic Jewish Law*, 1991. The next volume, *Conversion and Halakhic Pluralism* will be published soon. A Hebrew book, *The Sane Halakhah*, will be available in the autumn of 1993. An English translation is planned.

The Institute has conducted colloquia and seminars on Progressive *Halakhah* in four continents. Its Israeli editor regularly writes *halakhic* articles for the Israeli press and scholarly journals and has developed creative, liberal solutions to *halakhic* questions of marriage, conversion and personal status. We have affirmed the Jewishness of Ethiopian Jews and declared that they must not be forced to undergo conversion. We have publicly declared the egalitarian status of women in the synagogue and in public life. These and many other acts have helped to restore dignity and spirituality to Jewish religious life in Israel.

Moshe Zemer

ON THE AUTHORITY OF THE RABBI

Arnold Jacob Wolf

In the Jerusalem Talmud[1] we read: "He who sees a disciple of a sage who has died is as if he sees a scroll of the Torah that has been burned."

And in the same tractate we find:

"R. Jacob bar Abbaye in the name of R. Aha says: An elder who has forgotten his learning, because of an accident that happened to him, must be treated with the sanctity owed to the ark of the Torah."[2]

As Jacob Neusner has argued in many places, including his recent book *From Description to Conviction*,[3] this kind of statement seems to imply that the authority of the rabbi comes from his incarnating a holiness that is transferred from his learning to his person. Tales of the rabbis' behavior were exemplary, paradigmatic and even authoritative for the people. This model was extrapolated not only from what the rabbi taught but often from what the rabbi did. Supernatural power flowed from his mastering the dual Torah; the rabbi might be perceived as a kind of a Magian holy man, not only as a font of wisdom. The two were obviously connected. Respect due the Scroll was similarly due the master; Neusner believes that the Torah and the sage came to be identified with one another. Stories about sages had *halakhic* implications, though these were sometimes less than univocal. The authority of the rabbi proceeds from his knowledge of Torah but it often overflows the borders of mere intellectual mastery and becomes charismatic.

In later Judaism the personal authority of the rabbi becomes even more salient. Gershom Scholem has described the kind of rabbinic power that flows from mystical sources which the mere layperson cannot ever hope to achieve. If one needs a master to lead one in the paths of spiritual enlightenment, a kind of rabbinic guru, the master will have enormous personal authority as mediator of supernatural grace. There will emerge, finally in Hasidism most clearly, the *"rebbe"* or *"tzaddiq"* as indispensable mediator, the only conduit between the Jew and his or her God. Beyond any possible doubt, Judaism, in some of its formulations, knows the sacramental, meta-clerical, mysterious wonder-rabbi. Even as late as classical Reform Judaism, there is an echo of the intercessor-rabbi, functioning as a personal link with the Divine for his whole congregation. Some rabbis throughout our history have not only taught Torah, but have also claimed to become Torah, and were believed.

I have begun this introductory study with the charismatic claims of some rabbis because I do not believe charisma is decisive for rabbinic authority. Indeed, I consider it finally diversionary and potentially dangerous. Whether gnostic, Christian or indigenous in its origins and development, and however, powerful it may have been at various times in Jewish history, the idea of the sage as spiritual leader, mediator and personal standard has always been balanced or neutralized by another, very different model, one that I shall attempt to describe in the following pages.

"They sent word from there [*Eretz Yisrael*]: Take good care [to study] in company, and be heedful [not to neglect] the children of the poor, for from them Torah goeth forth, as it is written, The water shall flow out of his buckets [*mi-dalyaw*]: [meaning], from the *dallim* [poor] amongst them goeth forth Torah. And why is it not usual for scholars to give birth to sons who are scholars? - Said R. Joseph, That it might not be maintained the Torah is a mere legacy. R. Shisha, the son of R. Idi, said: That they should not be arrogant towards the community. R. Ashi said: Because they act high-handedly against the community. R. Ashi said: Because they call people asses. Rabina said: Because they do not first utter a blessing over the Torah."[4]

2

This passage is of great interest because it clearly shows that the authority of the sage derives exclusively from his learning. He is not the scion or progenitor of an aristocratic line (despite what we know about the family of Hillel the Elder); he is not allowed to act in a superior way to his fellow-Jews because he is one of them. He is not allowed to disparage less learned Jews, but is required to teach them. He must always bless the Torah before reading or teaching it, because his authority comes from it and not to it. He is, in short, a servant of the sacred, not its master.

In a strange passage Rabbi Hanina is punished for misrepresenting rabbinic status.

"R. Papa and R. Huna, son of R. Joshua, were once going along the road when they met R. Hanina, the son of R. Ika. They said to him: Now that we see you we make two blessings over you: 'Blessed be He who has imparted of His wisdom to them that fear Him,' and 'Who has kept us alive.' He said to them: I, also, on seeing you counted it as equal to seeing sixty myriads of Israel, but I made three blessings over you, those two, and 'Blessed is He that discerneth secrets.' They said to him: Are you so clever as all that? They cast their eyes on him and he died." [5]

Some commentators believe R. Hanina's sin was sarcasm, but I think it was hyperbole. Rabbis are to be respected for their learning, which is a gift of God, but not exalted above ordinary human stature. The rabbi is in possession of no deep "secrets" and it is potentially dangerous to think he is, as R. Hanina found out.

The problem of rabbinic authority appears concretely as the problem of unstable rabbinic consensus. If rabbis do not teach the same thing, how can they all be right - or any of them? If they seem to interpret the Written Torah according to their personal lights, how can they be trusted or even understood? Does not their interminable debate prove they are both fallible and untrustworthy?

3

A famous text deals directly with this issue:

"The masters of assemblies:" These are the disciples of the wise, who sit in manifold assemblies and occupy themselves with the Torah, some pronouncing unclean and others pronouncing clean, some prohibiting and others permitting, some disqualifying and others declaring fit.

"Should one say: How then can I learn Torah? Therefore the text adds: 'All are given from one Shepherd.' One God gave them; one leader uttered them from the mouth of the Lord of all creation, blessed be He; for it is written: 'And God spoke all these words.' Also do thou make thine ear like the hopper and get thee a perceptive heart to understand the words of those who pronounce clean, the words of those who prohibit and the words of those who permit, the words of those who disqualify and the words of those who declare fit." [6]

It is not (only) the School of Hillel or (only) the School of Shammai that speaks the words of the living God. Even though they disagree, they both are authentic teachers of the Torah. Perhaps one should say: Only together, despite their differences, even because of their differences, can they communicate the Divine word. The Written Torah is overdetermined; more comes from it than any one interpreter can adequately communicate. It is not the rabbi personally who has real authority, then, but the rabbinic process, the whole community living and dead and unborn.

What prerogatives accompany a rabbinic position? The Talmudic texts try to walk a fine line between making life impossible for a scholar if he has no economic privilege at all and, on the other hand, of allowing him to commit the sin of using the Torah as a means of economic and professional advancement. In the Babylonian Talmud we read:

4

"It was taught: 'That thou mayest love the Lord thy God and that thou mayest obey His voice, and that thou mayest cleave unto Him.' [This means] that one should not say, I will read Scripture that I may be called a sage; I will study, that I may be called rabbi; I will study, to be an Elder, and sit in assembly [of elders]. Learn out of love, and then honor will come in the end, as it is written: 'Bind them upon thy fingers, write them upon the table of thine heart;' and it is also said: 'Her ways are ways of pleasantness;' also: 'She is a tree of life to them that lay hold upon her, and happy is everyone that retaineth her.'

"R. Eliezer son of R. Zadok said: Do [good] deeds for the sake of their Maker, and speak of them for their own sake. Make not of them a crown wherewith to magnify thyself, nor a spade to dig with. And this follows *a fortiori*. If Belshazzar, who merely used the holy vessels which had been profaned, was driven from the world, how much more so one who makes use of the crown of the Torah!

"Raba said: A rabbinical scholar may assert, I am a rabbinical scholar; let my business receive first attention, as it is written: 'And David's sons were priests;' just as a priest receives [his portion] first, so does the scholar too. And whence do we know this of a priest? - Because it is written: 'Thou shalt sanctify him therefore, for he offereth the bread of thy God;' whereon the School of R. Ishmael taught: 'Thou shalt sanctify him' - in all matters pertaining to holiness; to be the first to commence [the reading of the Law], the first to pronounce the blessing, and first to receive a good portion.

"Raba said: A rabbinical scholar may even declare, I will not pay poll-tax."[7]

Certain professional privileges accompany the role of rabbi, including exemption from some taxation and some priority in business, but he must not expect that his scholarship privileges him above other Jews regularly or extravagantly. He must, of course, live, but not necessarily well. The Talmudic image of the rabbi is preeminently, I believe, of a student and a teacher, modestly but forthrightly offering his interpretation of Scripture, living among his brothers and sisters, not above them, sometimes conceived by them to be a superior type, but still normally required to work for a living outside of his rabbinic life and to compete as an interpreter of Torah with his fellow sages. His leadership depends upon his learning. He neither inherits nor commands his authority. He solicits it. He does not presume to any sacramental powers, since, in the strict sense, Judaism knows no sacraments. He must not condemn the less learned nor defer to them. His word is law if, and only if, he can convince the community of scholars and, ultimately, the community of living Jews that he is right. He is part of an unending process of interpretation and legislation, a process fraught with deeply religious significance, but he is only a small part. He is not more than a teacher, but in Judaism that is a very great deal indeed.

The personal character of the rabbi is, accordingly, not irrelevant, as we learn from a passage in the Babylonian Talmud:

"Isaac, of the School of R. Jannai, said: If one's colleagues are ashamed of his reputation, that constitutes a profanation of the Name. R. Nahman b. Isaac commented: If people say, May the Lord forgive so-and so. Abaye explained: As it was taught: 'And thou shalt love the Lord thy God;' i.e., that the Name of Heaven be beloved because of you. If someone studies Scripture and Mishnah, and attends on the disciples of the wise, is honest in business, and speaks pleasantly to persons, what do people then say concerning him? 'Happy the father who taught him Torah; happy the teacher who taught him Torah; woe the people who have not studied the Torah; for this man has studied the Torah - look how fine his ways are, how righteous his deeds!' Of him does Scripture say: 'And He said unto me: Thou art My servant, Israel, in whom I will be glorified.' But if someone studies Scripture and Mishnah, attends on the disciples of the wise, but is dishonest in business, and discourteous in his relations with people, what do people say about him? 'Woe to him who studied the Torah; woe to his father who taught him the Torah; woe to his teacher who taught him Torah!' This man studied Torah: Look, how corrupt are his deeds, how ugly his ways; of him Scripture says: 'In that men said of them: These are the people of the Lord, and are gone forth out of His land.'"[8]

The authority of the rabbi, his power, derives from mastery of the Torah, and therefore, he is obligated to live in such a way that he casts honor upon God's Name and upon God's Word. I do not believe that the Talmud means to imply that it is his character that authorizes him in the first place. Good behavior merely accompanies, or, at least, should accompany, his learning.

In medieval times a rabbi could be "defrocked" for reasons of scholarly incompetence, as we discover from a document from Italy in the sixteenth century:

"Rabbi so-and-so did not pay heed to the honour of the other rabbis, but only wished to create rabbis as if he were the prince and head of the entire exile. He did something which is not to be done, particularly in the present age, when there is no longer ordination [in the classical Talmudic sense] outside of the Land of Israel, but only appointment, and we are, so to speak, the mere spokesmen of the sages. For we read in the Talmud... R. Johanan said, 'Who is a scholar that is to be appointed over the public? One of whom one may ask the *halakhah* in any place and he responds, even in Tractate Kallah....' Therefore, everything which that person did is null and void *ab initio* and is without substance...and particularly so if the people of that community did not wish to have him, and that person is unworthy of being

7

appointed as a rabbi, for in so far as I know him, I have not heard anything from him but words of external wisdom and philosophy, of which it is said, 'and awesome are all those whom it has killed' - this refers to those students who have not gained as much knowledge of Torah as they should have, but still glorify themselves before the ignorant and the people of their town...."[9]

In Imola, at the same time, a rabbi was rejected by a community because he behaved immaturely, and in their view, high-handedly. Conflict between rabbinic authority and community power is a constant motif of medieval and early modern Judaism.[10] The rabbi had to know the texts he was teaching, but he also had to make it possible for his community to learn and to follow him; this meant that neither his character nor his style could be deeply objectionable.

In some communities, to be sure, charismatic spirituality was also much prized. An important Kabbalist in Italy clearly preferred a spiritually acute and mystically inclined rabbi to a pendant or even to a scholar:

"I will express myself briefly, why it is vanity to bring a cartload of [quotations] from the words of the authorities (*posqim*), as many as they be, both old and new, who composed books and many words, which are weariness to the flesh; for even if a man lived a thousand years twice over, it would be nearly impossible to exhaust their fullness, as was stressed sternly by the great Excellent Rabbi Elia da Genazzano, who wrote in his *Iggeret Hamudot* as follows: 'Behold, two evils were done to us in this exile. One, that they abandoned the source of living waters, the words of Kabbalah, which are prophecy, and dug for themselves broken wells or wells of clay, to seek after the philosophers, and they drowned in deep mire from which they cannot rise. And secondly, the many doubts which came about after the completion of the Talmud, which are a great reason to waste much time, for what difference does it make if I fulfill the *mitzvot* according to Maimonides, who codified them in clear and concise language, or if one fulfills them according to the *Mordekhai* or the *Semag* or the other authorities, study of which is more difficult and even deeper than study of the Talmud? Apart from this, there arose between them controversies, this one says thus, and that one says thus, and if it seemed in the eyes of the later ones (*aharonim*), that Maimonides was too brief on a certain subject, they ought to have written a commentary on his work, it being a general work, and that would have been sufficient. And not everyone who wishes to take upon himself the name [of scholar] may do so, and in this I praise those who dwell on the south-eastern extremity of the Ocean, of whom R. Obadiah of Bertinoro wrote that some of them [the Yemenites] came to Jerusalem, and they say that they have only one [*halakhic*] authority, and all of them are expert in it."[11]

The predominant model continued to be the scholar-teacher. One who could master the sources and then make decisions that were adequate and convincing was the ideal rabbinic candidate. In each generation, the scholar had, in principle, the same authority as the most revered of his predecessors. Each generation got the leadership it deserved; each generation should accept the leadership it had. A rabbi had to protect the honor of the Torah by protecting his own prerogatives. He had to stand up for his own rights, because he was, and only because he was, a representative of the scholarly discipline.

"An outstanding scholar is one who was ordained to teach the entire Torah, for Jephthah in his generation is like Samuel in his generation; even if there is one greater than he in his generation, so long as there is no one greater in his city, he is still called an outstanding scholar. Therefore, the sage takes precedence, and he ought to be called up first to the Torah.

"But if the scholar wished to forgo his honour at any time,

he may do so, as we have learned: 'The rabbi who waived his honour, his honour is waived,' but his disciples must nevertheless show him respect. But he may not be called up following the elder, because of the saying of R. Johanan, 'Every scholar who allows an ignoramus - even if he be the high priest - to bless before him is culpable of death, as is written, 'and those who hate Me loved death' - do not read 'those who hate Me' but 'those who make Me hated' - those who shame the Torah and make it hateful in the eyes of the people, allowing an ignoramus to be called up before him.' It is therefore fitting that that sage ought to minimize such forfeiture of honours, lest they come - Heaven forfend - to minimize the honour of Torah, [which] is very great."[12]

We cannot enter here into the complicated question of rabbinic ordination. Suffice it to say that rabbis made rabbis; scholars authorized their own successors. There could be no other way to become a rabbi than long apprenticeship under a master teacher. Rabbis were made, not born or set apart by sacraments. A typical, and most impressive medieval t'udah may appropriately conclude our necessarily sketchy, overview of rabbinic authority:

"Text of the Ordination granted by R. Isaac ben Emmanuel de Lattes to R. Samuel Kazani.

"I have seen you as a venerable old student, who has imbibed of the breasts of Mother Wisdom, and been weaned on the milk of the Torah, and you have arrived at [the level of] instruction, and if you prevent yourself from doing so, Heaven forfend, you enter into the category of those of whom it is said 'for it has felled many corpses.' And a good thing was done in its time by the Gaon and Exalted Rabbi, who sits on the throne of teaching, Rabbi Samuel, son of the Gaon Meir Katzenellenbogen, who came to enjoy the mitzvah of adorning you with the crown of the rabbinate, and I will come after his honour to join him and be joined with him in this matter. And from the day that you came to

Venice and brought forth pearls from your mouth, I have judged you to be a sharp person, who pursues justice and seeks truth, and you have found favour in my eyes, to be the judge upon the earth within the congregation of God. And if you have set your heart to know the science of healing, and for this reason you have lifted up your hand, the weak hand, the left of every person, in external wisdoms, you have not withheld yourself from studying much Torah, and the right hand of God, the Torah of God which is perfect with you, does mightily - the right hand of God is uplifted, and a golden bowl - for you have given to the crown of the Torah and added quality, that is the ruling mistress, and you have made the other wisdoms as handmaidens which serve it, as they have been placed under your hand. And the diligence which was in your hand for the beautification of Torah, shall uplift you, and you shall sit upon the throne of kings - 'and who are the kings? The rabbis.' You shall stand in the place of the great [ones], for behold I come to you, your honour, Rabbi Samuel Kazani, son of our rabbi, the wise man, Shabbetai, may he long live, of Candia. And lay on my hand, and add light to your light, to be called 'Rabbi' in all matters pertaining to holiness, and there shall be placed in your hands the garments of rabbis: a stick and a whip with which to beat those deserving of it by the needs of the hour; a *shofar* with which to excommunicate every man who rebels against you, by your ordinances and limitations to add further limitations to the sanctions of the Torah to those that the Torah has given us in matters of forbidden and permitted; a shoe to perform *halizah*; and a quill with which to correct divorces and to issue judgement and to rule in marital issues, for you are expert in their nature. And who shall teach knowledge or explicit traditions when the heads of the people are gathered together in the holy congregation with them, your honour shall be with them and amongst them you shall be counted, for such is befitting to you. For the above-mentioned Rabbi Samuel is fit to be a righteous teacher and to do justice and righteousness in the land, and with mercy shall his seat be established forever, and he shall live long in his kingdom. Amen."

11

(Isaac Joshua b. R. Emmanuel de Lattes Ferrara, 12 Nissan 5329 [1569])[13]

Notes

1. J. Moed Qatan 3.7; see also S.S. Cohon, "Authority in Judaism," HUCA 11, Cincinnati, 1936, pp. 593 ff.

2. *Ibid.*, 3.1.

3. Jacob Neusner: *From Description to Conviction*, Atlanta, 1987, Chapter 3.

4. B. Nedarim 81a.

5. B. Berakhot 58b.

6. B. Hagigah 3b.

7. B. Nedarim 62b.

8. B. Yoma 86a.

9. See Robert Bonfil: *Rabbis and Jewish Communities in Renaissance Italy*, Oxford, 1990, pp. 53ff. Quoting R. Jacob Israel Finzi, *T'shuvot"* Sect. 164. See the Hebrew edition of Bonfil's book, Document 3, pp. 215-216. *HaRabbanut B'italiah Bi T'kufot Harenesans*, Jerusalem, 5739.

10. See A.J. Wolf in *Encyclopedia of Religion*, 12, 181ff.

11. Bonfil, p. 265, quoting R. Abraham da Sant Angelo. The text appears in Yacov Boksenboim, *T'shuvot Matanot Ba-adam*, Tel Aviv, 1983 Sect. 39, p. 88.

12. Bonfil, p. 56, quoting R. Aharon ben Israel Finzi, from Ms Jerusalem, yMakhon Ben-Zvi, #4040, Sect. 5.

13. *Ibid.*, p. 326ff. from *T'shuvot R. Yitzhaq MiLattes*, ii, Fo. 128, published in the Hebrew edition of Bonfil, Document #8, R. 222.

K'VOD HARAV

Honor Due a Rabbi

Bernard M. Zlotowitz

K'vod harav has deep roots in Judaism. As the rabbis teach: "The fear of your rabbi shall be like the fear of Heaven."[1] They deduced this principle from the equation in the Biblical verse "...honor the face of the old man, and fear your God...."[2]

The Talmud understood old man, *zaqen*, to be either a man of 70 years of age,[3] or one who has acquired wisdom: "Our rabbis taught: 'You shalt rise up before the hoary head;' I might think, even before an aged sinner; therefore it is said, 'and honor the face of a *zaqen*,' and *zaqen* can only refer to a Sage, for it is said, 'Gather to Me seventy men of the elders of Israel.'[4] Rabbi Jose, the Galilean, said *zaqen* (means) only him who has acquired wisdom (reading *zaqen* as an abbreviation, *zeh qanah hokhmah*), for it is said, The Lord possessed me (sc. wisdom personified) 'as the beginning of His way.'"[5] Thus, the Talmud interpreted *zaqen*, as one who has acquired wisdom, to mean a rabbi.

The admonition to fear the Lord, and by extension the rabbi, was to be taken very seriously. Failure to respect the rabbi could result in excommunication, or even death. The curse of a rabbi was no trifling matter:

"Warm yourself by the fire of wise men, but beware of their coals, lest you be singed, for their bite is the bite of a fox and their sting is the sting of a scorpion, while their hiss is the hiss of a serpent."[6]

The power of this statement is concretized in a dispute that took place between Rabbi Eliezer and his student, Rabbi Akiva. Rabbi Akiva mocked his teacher in a disagreement as to whether ancillary activities are permitted on Shabbat in the Temple, such as sharpening knives and preparing fuel, along with slaughtering animals. Rabbi Eliezer permitted it. Rabbi Akiva did not. As a result, Rabbi Eliezer cursed his student: "Akiva, you have refuted me by *shehitah*; by *shehitah* shall be your (lit. his) death!"[7]

It seems astonishing that a teacher should have cursed a student so severely, especially an outstanding one, for refuting him publicly on an *halakhic* issue. A milder rebuke would have been sufficient. This leads us to search for a precedent for such reaction in the Torah. When Moses hit the rock, instead of speaking to it, God punished him by preventing him from entering the Promised Land,[8] and having him die on Mt. Nebo,[9] just before the Israelites were to enter and conquer Canaan. Even the Midrashic account of Moses pleading to let him enter as a roaming beast of the field or a bird in flight does not move God or cause Him to change His mind.[10]

Moses' sin was taken as a failure of *k'vod harav*; i.e. failing to grant proper honor to his teacher, the *Ribbono Shel Olam*, by not sanctifying His name. The same is true in the great model of Rabbi Akiva, who equally did not render proper respect to his teacher, Rabbi Eliezer. Thus, in both cases, that is, of Moses and Rabbi Akiva, the adage applies that the mightier they are, the greater they fall, or, to use the Biblical phrase: "How are the mighty fallen!"[11]

On closer examination of the relationship between Rabbi Eliezer and Rabbi Akiva, it appears that this was not the only time they had clashed over an *halakhic* interpretation and that Rabbi Akiva publicly, over and over again, embarrassed his teacher.

14

In a dispute over what is permitted and prohibited in the preparation for a Sabbath *brit milah*, Rabbi Akiva contended that that which can be prepared prior to the Sabbath cannot be prepared on the Sabbath.[12] Rabbi Eliezer disagreed, teaching that anything and everything may be done, even chopping wood to make charcoal for forging the circumcision knife.[13] Rabbi Eliezer presumably no longer could abide the "disrespect" of his student, sparking his furious condemnation.

It should be noted that so strident and implacable was Rabbi Eliezer in pressing his views that eventually he was condemned and excommunicated by his colleagues, even though his interpretation was correct. Rabbi Akiva's role in the following dispute drove a further wedge between teacher and student:

"If he cut it [an oven] into separate tiles, placing sand between each tile: Rabbi Eliezer declared it clean and the sages declared it unclean....On that day Rabbi Eliezer brought forward every imaginable argument, but they did not accept them. Said he to them: 'If the *halakhah* agrees with me, let this carob-tree prove it!' Thereupon the carob-tree was torn a hundred cubits out of its place - others affirm, four hundred cubits. 'No proof can be brought from a carob-tree,' they retorted. Again he said to them: 'If the *halakhah* agrees with me, let the stream of water prove it!' Whereupon the stream of water flowed backwards. 'No proof can be brought from a stream of water,' they rejoined. Again he urged: 'If the *halakhah* agrees with me, let the walls of the schoolhouse prove it!' Thereupon the walls inclined to the point of falling. But Rabbi Joshua rebuked them, saying, 'When scholars are engaged in a *halakhic* dispute, what have you to interfere?' Hence they did not fall, in honor of Rabbi Joshua, [and] in honor of Rabbi Eliezer they are standing thus inclined. Again he said to them: 'If the *halakhah* agrees with me, let it be proved from Heaven!' Whereupon a Heavenly voice cried out: 'Why do you dispute with Rabbi Eliezer seeing that in all matters the *halakhah* agrees with him!' But Rabbi Joshua arose and exclaimed: 'It is not in heaven.[14] What did he mean by this? - Said Rabbi Jeremiah: 'After the Torah was given at Mt. Sinai; we pay no attention to a Heavenly Voice, because Thou hast long since written in the Torah at Mt. Sinai: After the majority must one incline....'"[15]

Though we have here a case where rabbinical authority supersedes heavenly authority, nevertheless, God does not seem to resent it. On the contrary, God seems to sanction the unlimited authority of the rabbis to interpret the law. The Gemara emphasizes that once God gave the Torah to the Jews at Sinai, all legal interpretations rested in the hands of the rabbis, even if they err in judgement.

Returning to the conflict between Rabbi Eliezer, on the one hand, and Rabbi Akiva and the rabbis, one the other hand, the Talmud offers the following account:

"Rabbi Nathan met Elijah and asked him: 'What did the Holy One, Blessed be He, do in that hour?' -- He laughed [with joy], he replied, saying: 'My sons have defeated Me! My sons have defeated Me!' It was said: On that day all objects which Rabbi Eliezer had declared clean were brought and burnt in fire [as unclean]. They then took a vote and excommunicated him. Said they: 'Who shall go and inform him?' 'I will go,' answered Rabbi Akiva, 'lest an unsuitable person go and inform him, and thus destroy the whole world.' What did Rabbi Akiva do? He donned black garments and wrapped himself in black, and sat a distance of four cubits from him. 'Akiva,' Rabbi Eliezer said to him, 'what has particularly happened today?' 'Master,' he replied, 'it appears to me that your companions hold aloof from you.' Thereupon he, too, rent his garments, took off his shoes, removed [his seat], and sat on the earth, while tears streamed from his eyes. The world was then smitten [with the destruction of] a third of the olive crop, a third

16

of the wheat, and a third of the barley crop. Some say: The dough in women's hands swelled up."[16]

In another encounter between Rabbi Akiva and Rabbi Eliezer we learn that during a drought in *Eretz Yisrael* a fast was declared and Rabbi Eliezer pleaded with God to send rain, but to no avail. Rabbi Akiva then stepped down before the *Aron HaKodesh*[17] and prayed:

"Our Father, our King, we have no King but You. Our Father, our King, for Your sake have mercy upon us," and rain fell.[18]

The rabbis viewed this miracle as a sign that God preferred Rabbi Akiva to Rabbi Eliezer. The Gemara attempts to correct this impression by declaring: "...a Heavenly Voice was heard proclaiming, [the prayer of] this man [Rabbi Akiva] was answered, not because he is greater than the other man, but because he is ever forbearing and the other is not."[19] However, Rabbi Eliezer was not assuaged. In an attempt to mitigate Rabbi Eliezer's anger, pain and anguish, Rabbi Akiva offered the following analogy: "There was a king who had two daughters, one beautiful and one ugly. Whenever the beautiful daughter came to request something, he kept her in his presence as long as possible, delaying his response so as to keep her in his sight. Whenever his ugly daughter wanted something, he approved, even before she entered the throne room, so as to avoid looking at her."[20]

Rabbi Eliezer's multiple humiliations ultimately sealed Rabbi Akiva's fate. Rabbi Eliezer no longer could take the disrespect his student heaped upon him. The curse Rabbi Eliezer uttered against Rabbi Akiva was not idle talk. It had power. As Scripture declares: "...the land cannot contain all His words."[21]

Taken as a whole from the incidents cited, Rabbi Akiva

seems to have had a perverse joy, (perhaps a sado/masochistic personality) in discrediting his teacher, Rabbi Eliezer, - even offering to be the bearer of bad tidings - notwithstanding his own statement that if an unsuitable person went to inform him the world would be destroyed. The end result was that Rabbi Akiva did not mitigate the pain of Rabbi Eliezer. On the contrary, Rabbi Eliezer was so deeply hurt that his pain had powerful repercussions on the populace in that one third of the crop failed.

Equally tragic was the case of Resh Laqish, who was punished by Rabbi Yohanan for showing lack of respect for his teacher. Resh Laqish disagreed with his teacher, Rabbi Yohanan, regarding when certain instruments are susceptible to ritual uncleanness.

"Feeling deeply hurt, Rabbi Yohanan censured[22] his student, and Resh Laqish fell deathly ill. Rabbi Yohanan's sister, the wife of Resh Laqish, pleaded with her brother to forgive her husband: 'Forgive him for the sake of my son....' Rabbi Yohanan replied: 'Leave your fatherless children. I will preserve them alive....'[23] 'For the sake of my widowhood! And let your widows trust in me...'[24] he assured her. But despite her pleas, Resh Laqish died. As a result, Rabbi Yohanan inconsolable and guilt-ridden, fell into a deep depression. The rabbis prayed for his death, hoping thereby to bring him peace of mind."[25]

In another incident a boor was excommunicated for insulting a rabbi: "A certain man from Nehardea entered a butcher's shop in Pumbeditha and demanded, 'Give me meat!' 'Wait until Rabbi Judah ben Ezekiel's attendant takes his,' was the reply, 'and then we will serve you.' 'Who is Judah ben Shewiskel [a contemptuous mispronunciation of Ezekiel, meaning the glutton], to take precedence over me and be served before me?' When Rabbi Judah was told of the insult, he pronounced a ban against the man...and proclaimed him a slave."[26] The man brought a suit against Rabbi Judah, but lost his case. During the trial, however, the presiding judge, Rabbi Nahman, asked Rabbi Judah why he did not flog the man, as was his custom. "Because he insulted me through my attendant," responded Rabbi Judah, "I dealt with him more severely."[27] Thus, various forms of punishment were meted out for insulting a rabbi or his servants.

Respect for a rabbi was deemed so absolute that even a person with a legitimate complaint was obligated to suppress even negative thoughts about the offending rabbi. The Mishnah relates that after the death sentence had been imposed on a person found guilty of a capital crime by a rabbinical court and the sentence had been carried out, the relatives "came and greeted the judges and the witnesses as if to say, 'We have naught against you in our hearts, for you have judged the judgement of truth.'"[28]

The rabbis were uncompromising in demanding respect. The rabbis could never renounce their honor. "Rabbi Isaac ben Shila said in Rabbi Mattena's name in the name of Rabbi Hisda: If a father renounces the honour due to him, it is renounced; but if a rabbi renounces his honour it is not renounced."[29]

The rabbis' honor was even to supersede that of a father. If there was to be a choice, the student must honor his teacher over his father: "A man is required to honor and fear his teacher [i.e. rabbi], more than his father, for his father brings him life in this world and his teacher brings him life in the world to come."[30]

To this point we have basically discussed a student disrespecting his rabbi, and the penalties imposed. But what are the consequences of a congregant, or a community, acting disrespectfully toward a rabbi? Rabbi Chaim Yosef David Azulai (1724-1806) was asked by the leaders of the Jewish community whether they had to abide by the instructions left by their deceased

19

rabbi, who had stipulated in his will that none of his titles or laudatory attributes be mentioned at his funeral, and that no tombstone be placed on his grave. The leaders felt that it would be disrespectful to their rabbi to carry out his last will and testament.

Rabbi Azulai responded that the deceased rabbi's request not to mention his titles and deeds had to be honored, because in all probability "his intention was to gain atonement by concealing his praises, 'for there is not a righteous man on earth who does good and never sins.'"[31] The request that no tombstone be placed on the rabbi's grave should be ignored however, for according to Ari (Rabbi Isaac Luria), "this brings about the restoration for the soul." Had the deceased rabbi remembered that teaching, he presumably would not have put the tombstone ban in his will.[32]

Thus there are times when, for the sake of a rabbi's soul, his wishes have to be ignored. But this may be done only after careful deliberation.

In return for the respect accorded the rabbis, the rabbis for their part had to behave in a decorous manner in their relationship to the community.

A rabbi was not permitted to do manual labor in the presence of three people. When Rabbi Judah came to Rabbi Huna to ask him a question, he saw him constructing a railing to the roof of his house.[33] Rabbi Judah inquired of Rabbi Nahman, "Do you not accept Rabbi Huna ben Idi's dictum in Samuel's name: Once a man is appointed head of a community, he may not do [manual] labor in the presence of three?"[34]

The rabbi must not conduct himself frivolously.[35] The Talmud teaches that there are six things unbecoming of a *talmid haham* [rabbi]: "He should not go abroad perfumed; he should not go out at night alone; he should not go abroad in patched sandals; he should not converse with a woman in the street; he should not recline at a meal in the company of ignorant persons; and he should not be the last to enter the *Bet HaMidrash*. Some add that he should not take long strides or walk haughtily."[36]

The Gemara [37] elaborates: "That he not go out wearing perfume; i.e., with a fragrance on his clothes, for it signals an interest in a homosexual liaison; that he not go out alone at night, to avoid being suspected of seeking to engage in immoral practices. If, however, it is his custom to go out at night and keep a fixed appointment and the people know this, it is permitted. A scholar should never appear shabbily dressed in public, and should not converse with a woman in the street [including his wife, daughter and sister] 'because not everyone knows who are his female relatives.' He ought not dine with an ignoramus, so as not to be 'drawn into their ways.' He must not be the last to enter the *Bet Ha Midrash*, so as not to be regarded a laggard pushing his way through the crowd, 'stepping over the heads of a holy people.'[38] He should not take long strides because 'long strides diminish a man's eyesight by a five hundredth part.'[39] Finally, the prohibition against walking haughtily reflects the rabbinic notion that by so walking the rabbi 'pushes against the heels of the Divine Presence, since it is written, "The whole earth is full of His Glory;"[40] i.e., that God's presence is manifest in the universe. The very act of walking manifests a certain dignity and, therefore, the rabbi must conduct himself so as not to bring discredit upon himself.

One of the predominant themes of the above passage in Berakhot is that the rabbi must be aware of "what people would say" (*ma-arit ayin*). Like Caesar's wife, the rabbi had to be above suspicion. He always had to be conscious of his status, avoiding any situation that might compromise that status.

Part of the rabbi's responsibility is to be competent, because

21

one should not honor the incompetent. The rabbis taught: "If the scholar is a worthy person, learn from him and do not shun him, but if he is not, destroy him and cut him down."[41]

The *Shita Mekubetzet* of Rabbi Betzalel Ashkenazi (1520?-1594?), ruled that if a rabbi is incompetent in his knowledge of the Torah, he may be removed from his position [and this does not come under the category of disrespect for the rabbi]. If such action is taken during the term of the contract, "...the congregation is free of any guilt. On the contrary, they are to be commended for removing an unqualified person from the rabbinate. In so doing, they raise the banner of the Torah....It is plain as day that the congregation is innocent and blameless...."[42]

The rabbis held their honor very dear, even reinterpreting the word "God" in a biblical verse to mean judge [rabbi]. "'You shall not revile God'[43]...say our rabbis. It once happened that a man came before a judge who pronounced the verdict in his favor. He then went about saying: 'There is no judge like this one in the whole world.' Later he again came before the same judge, but this time the ruling went against him. So he went about saying: 'There is no greater idiot of a judge than this one.' People then said to him - how yesterday the judge could be splendid and today an idiot? The rabbinical response: On this account the Bible exhorts you: 'You shall not revile God (i.e. the judges/rabbis).' The punishment, a poor harvest."[44]

In addition, to protect their rights and privileges, the rabbis ruled themselves exempt from taxes.[45] It is important to note that rabbis derived their income from various professions or crafts, (e.g. physicians, sandlers, etc.), but received no remuneration for their rabbinical duties and thus insisted on their rights to tax exemption.

In the final analysis, the rabbis guarded their status and

position zealously, demanding due respect even over and above the Torah: "How foolish are those who stand up before the Scroll of the Law and not before a great man!"[46] Those rabbis who would forgo the honor due them (though they were forbidden to do so) suffered the ridicule of their colleagues: "A rabbi who surrenders the respect due to him is no longer respected."[47]

Thus, *k'vod harav* is a double-edged sword in that if one is disrespectful to his teacher one invites disrespect for himself as a teacher. If one behaves in an indecorous manner as a rabbi one brings the role of the rabbi into disrepute. If one is incompetent in the role itself one makes the role meaningless. The honor of the rabbi is connected to fear of God. We, who teach Torah, are the vehicle for our people to come to God. If we act in such a way we fulfill the verse - honor the face of the *zaqen* - the rabbi - and fear your God.

Notes

1. Ethics of the Fathers 4.15.

2. Leviticus 19.32.

3. Ethics of the Fathers 5.24.

4. Numbers 11.16.

5. Proverbs 8.22; Qiddushin 32b.

6. Ethics of the Fathers 2.15.

7. M. Pesahim 6.1; B. Pesahim 69a (see also Louis Finkelstein, *Akiba, Scholar, Saint and Martyr*, Northvale, NJ and London, 1990, pp. 92-93). Apparently the martyrdom of Akiva is the result of Eliezer's curse, more than from defying the Roman edict prohibiting the study of the Torah, if we accept the Talmudic belief that words have power.

The *halakhah* that a student who renders a rabbinic decision in the presence of his teacher is worthy of death (*hayiv mitah*) (B. Eruvin 63a), may be an outgrowth of a dispute between teacher and student. Thus, in order to avoid the kind of tragic consequences described in this paper, the rabbis felt that the better course of valor was to remain silent. As the *pereq* teaches, *s'yag lahokhmah sh'tiqah* - "The fence to wisdom is silence" (3.17). This requires further investigation.

8. Numbers 20.1-13. In Exodus 17.1-7. Moses, in a similar situation, is told to hit the rock. See also W. Gunther Plaut (ed.) *The Torah, A Modern Commentary,* New York, 1981, pp. 1155-1156.

9. Deuteronomy 32.48-52.

10. Deuteronomy Rabbah 11.10.

11. II Samuel 1.19.

12. B. Shabbat 133a; B. Yevamot 14a; M. Pesahim 6.2 and M. Menahot 11.3.

13. B. Shabbat 130a and B. Yevamot 14a.

14. Deuteronomy 30.12.

15. Exodus 23.2; B. Baba Metzia 59a & b. The actual Biblical quotation reads: "Do not follow a multitude to do evil." Rabbi Jeremiah's quotation, however, conveys the sense that the majority rules.

16. *Ibid.,* 59b.

17. In Talmudic times and in many Orthodox synagogues in Eastern Europe the pulpit stood below the Ark in fulfillment of the verse, "Out of the depths have I called Thee" (Psalms 130.1).

18. B. Ta-anit 25b.

19. *Ibid.,* 25b.

20. J. Ta-anit 3.4, 66c. See also Louis Finkelstein, *op. cit.,* pp. 105-106.

21. Amos 7.10.

22. The verb is missing in the Gemara but the sense calls for censuring or cursing.

23. Jeremiah 49.11.

24. *Ibid.*, 49.11.

25. B. Baba Metzia 84a.

26. B. Qiddushin 70a.

27. *Ibid.*, 70a and b.

28. M. Sanhedrin 6.6.

29. B. Qiddushin 32a.

30. *Kitzur Shulhan Arukh* 144.1; See also *Shulhan Arukh*, Yoreh Deah 242.1.

31. Ecclesiastes 7.20.

32.   *Teshuvot Haim Shaal*, Lemberg, 1886, part 1, #71.6; cf. Avraham Yaakov Finkel, *The Responsa Anthology*, Northvale, NJ and London, 1990, p.121.

33. Deuteronomy 22.8.

34. B. Qiddushin 70a.

35. Rambam, *Hilhot Sandhedrin* 25.3.

36. B. Berakhot 43b.

37. *Ibid.*, 43b.

38. In addition to B. Berakhot 43b see also B. Yevamot 105b and B. Qiddushin 33a. In the latter citation the rabbi is cautioned to avoid crowds so as not to trouble the people by having them rise from their seats as a token of respect when they see him coming.

39. B. Berakhot 43b.

40. Isaiah 6.31; B. Berakhot 43b. It is interesting to note that the Pharisees believed that there was no physical manifestation of God, whereas the Sadducees believed that there was. The difference of opinion focuses on the interpretation of Leviticus 16.2, "...for I appear in the cloud over the cover." The Sadducees contended that the High Priest could not enter the Holy of Holies until the shrine was filled with smoke so that upon entering he would not see God and die. The Pharisees, on the other hand, contended that since God had no physical manifestation, the High Priest could enter the Holy of Holies, confirm that the shrine did not contain the physical manifestation of God, and then fill the room with smoke (see Yoma 19b).

41. B. Ta-anit 7a.

42. *Teshuvot Rabbi Betzalel Ashkenazi*, Jerusalem, 1968, #24, cf. in Avraham Yaakov Finkel, *op. cit.*, p. 75.

43. Exodus 22.27.

44. Exodus Rabba 31.8.

45. B. Baba Batra 8a.

46. B. Makot 22b.

47. B. Qiddushin 32a: This is how Reuven Alcalay *Words of the Wise*, Jerusalem-Ramat Gan, 1970, p. 412 paraphrases the statement in the Gemara, *harav shemahal al k'vodo, k'vodo mahul.*

The Talmudic translations, with modifications, in this paper are either from Herbert Danby, *The Mishnah*, London 1933 or Rabbi Dr. I. Epstein (ed.), *The Babylonian Talmud*, London, 1948.

THE PROFESSIONALIZATION OF THE RABBINATE
in the Talmud and the *Halakhic* Commentaries of Rambam and Karo

Richard Rheins

The modern rabbinate, with its array of professional organizations, pension plans, tenured positions and complex contracts, hardly seems concerned with the *halakhic* justification for rabbinic salaries and financial compensation. And yet, the question of whether the office of rabbi should be an unpaid position or one entitled to financial emoluments was once the center of a passionate *halakhic* debate. By reviewing *halakhic* evidence for the "professionalization" of the rabbinate, we can gain both a greater understanding for the foundations of the modern rabbinate, as well as an appreciation for the courage and insight of our sages as they employed *halakhic* principles in order to span the gap between an ethical ideal and a moral responsibility.

It is popularly held that the office of rabbi originally was strictly an honorary position and that rabbis did not receive salaries prior to the fourteenth century.[1] If it is true that, as Ephraim Urbach states: 'The acceptance of remuneration from the public was forbidden,"[2] then how did the later rabbis justify their salaries and fees? What is the *halakhic* foundation of the professional rabbinate?

In order to understand the key *halakhic* issues that affected the development of the professional rabbinate, we will first examine several Talmudic passages which address the question of awarding financial compensation and benefits to the earliest sages and rabbis.[3] Second, we will turn to the twelfth century comments of one of the last great authorities who opposed rabbinic salaries, Moses Maimonides (Rambam). His remarks, quoted at length, effectively sharpen the focus of the *halakhic* debate. Finally, we will see how Joseph Karo justified the professional rabbinate in opposition to Rambam's position.

For the purpose of this paper, a "professional rabbi" is defined as: "one who receives financial compensation and benefits in support of his rabbinic vocation."[4]

THE PROFESSIONAL RABBINATE AS EVIDENCED IN THE TALMUD[5]

Contrary to "popular opinion," the traditions preserved in the Talmud do not universally prohibit rabbinic salaries, fees and benefits. True, some authorities such as Hillel and Rabbis Zadok and Tarfon were opposed to deriving benefit from teaching Torah,[6] but others (Judah, Assi and Raba)[7] established the *halakhic* foundations for financial compensation, communal salaries and other benefits.

It is important to begin with a review of those Talmudic passages which are most frequently cited in *halakhic* literature in relationship to the issues of rabbinic compensation, salaries and benefits. Below, the passages have been divided into two major groupings: 1) Talmudic traditions which prohibit salaries and limit privileges; and 2) Talmudic traditions which permit financial compensation and privileges.

1. The Talmudic Traditions which Prohibit Salaries and Limit Privileges

Two passages are frequently cited by those authorities in opposition to rabbinic salaries, fees and benefits:[8]

"R. Zadok said: Do not make [the Torah] a crown to make yourself great, nor a spade with which to dig." "And Hillel used to say: He who makes worldly use of the crown [of the Torah] shall

THE PROFESSIONALIZATION OF THE RABBINATE

perish." From this you learn that whoever uses the words of the Torah for his own benefit will cause his own destruction.[9]

If one takes payment (sekhar) to act as a judge: his judgements are void; to give evidence, his evidence is void; to sprinkle[10] or to sanctify, the waters are considered cave waters and the ashes are considered only ordinary ashes.[11]

Gemara: Where is it proved [that one may not take payment for teaching the Torah and rendering decisions]? R. Judah reported in the name of Rav: "Scripture says: 'Behold I have taught you laws and statutes....'[12] Just as I teach you gratuitously, so you should teach gratuitously."[13]

The passages above delineate a clear position against the acceptance of salaries (sekhar) for rabbis. Hillel's statement was understood to prohibit someone from earning a livelihood or deriving material advantage from his expertise of the Torah.[14] The d'rash of Deuteronomy 4.5, in B. Bekhorot 29a, established the ideal of teaching the Torah for free because God gave the Torah to us for free. This interpretation became an often cited anthem for those authorities who sought to prohibit financial compensation for the rabbis. The Talmud also preserves traditions that are opposed to judges who are in the habit of borrowing.[15] Some authorities, Rabbi Tarfon, for example, were most extreme in their refusal to benefit from their Torah scholarship. Tarfon grieved all his lifetime because he had once saved his own life by informing an attacker that he was a rabbi.[16]

2. Talmudic Passages which Permit Financial Compensation and Privileges

Notwithstanding the above mentioned prohibitions against rabbinic salaries and benefits, the Talmud also contains several traditions which permit:

29

a) compensation for "time and trouble"
b) tax exemptions
c) business advantages
d) salaries from communal funds.

Below, we will examine each of these areas of rabbinic support.

A) Compensation for "time and trouble"

While payment for the performance of a *mitzvah* is technically prohibited,[17] the Talmud does establish the foundation for rabbinic compensation through the principles of *sekhar batalah* and *tirha*.

Sekhar batalah and *sekhar tirha* [also referred to by its Aramaic equivalent, *agar batalah*] is compensation for the loss of time. In theory, a rabbi would "normally" earn a living by means of a secular occupation. Whenever he took time off from his occupation in order to perform some rabbinic function, the rabbi would suffer a loss of wages. The principle of *sekhar batalah* and *sekhar tirhah* empowered the rabbi to demand just compensation for his lost wages. A good example of this is found in the following:

"Karna used to take one *istira* from the innocent party and one *istira* from the guilty party. But how could he act in such a manner? Is it not written in Scripture, And thou shall take no gift...."[18] But this applies only where he [the judge] takes [the gift] as a bribe, but Karna took [the money] as a fee (*agra*). But is it permissible [for a judge to take money] as a fee? Have we not in fact learned that the legal decisions of one who takes a fee for acting as judge are null and void?[19] This applies only to a fee for pronouncing judgement, while Karna was only taking compensation for loss of work (*agar bateilah*)."[20]

Karna earned a living as a wine-tester. Therefore, he could demand his wine-tester's wages when he was called away to perform a rabbinic function.

Another form of compensation was recompense for *tirha* (the physical labor or "trouble" required in preparation for a *mitzvah*). In the following passage, note that the Mishnah could be understood to permit the payment of fees. The Gemara, however, explains the fees as compensation for *tirha*:

"If one takes payment for inspecting the firstlings, they must not be slaughtered by his instructions, unless he was an expert (*mumheh*) like Ila in Yavneh whom the sages permitted to accept four Roman coins for small cattle and six for large cattle, whether they were unblemished or blemished.[21]

Gemara: What is the reason? In one case (i.e., with the large cattle) he has much trouble (*tirhah*), whereas in the other case (i.e., the small cattle) he does not have much trouble."[22]

In the above case the Gemara draws a fine line in order to justify the acceptance of fees. Still mindful of the prohibition forbidding fees for performing a religious act, the Gemara contends that Ila received his fees because of the physical difficulty of handling animals, but not for the *mitzvah* of the inspection. Thus the officiant's duties are separated into two categories:

a) the physical labor required in preparation for the *mitzvah*
b) the performance of the religious act or *mitzvah* itself.

One could thereby receive compensation for the non-religious functions involved in the preparation for a *mitzvah*.[23]

The establishment of these two forms of compensation, *sekhar batalah* and *tirha*, effectively laid the groundwork of the

31

halakhic justification for rabbinic fees.

B) *Rabbinic tax and business benefits*

We have already learned how the Talmud *halakhically* justified certain fees and payments to the rabbis. But *sekhar batalah* and *tirha* can be seen as compensations for loss and not actual benefits. However, special rights and privileges were granted to the rabbis, for example, the benefit of tax-exemption.[24]

In order to extend their rights and benefits, the rabbis, as depicted in the Talmud, were understood to be the natural inheritors of the privileges previously belonging to the Temple priests.[25] The following passages link the rights and privileges of the rabbis to those of the *kohanim* (the Temple priests):

"Rabbi Yonah gave tithes to Rabbi Acha bar 'Ulla, not because he was a priest but because he studied the Torah."[26]

"Raba said, "A rabbinical scholar may assert, I am a rabbinical scholar; let my business receive first attention, as it is written, 'And David's sons were *kohanim* [of course, David's sons were not *kohanim*, but this verse in II Samuel 8:18, simply is used to show that just as David's sons received priestly privileges, though they were not priests, so, too, should rabbis receive priestly privileges;'[27]; just as a priest receives first, so does the scholar receive first." And from where do we know that a priest receives first? Because it is written, 'Thou shall sanctify him; for he offers the bread of thy God.'"[28]

The benefit of tax-emption was defended staunchly. Rabbi Nahman ben Isaac even declared that the right of rabbis to exemption from poll-taxes was *d'oraita* (Biblical) and not simply a rabbinic ruling.[29] The following passage shows to what lengths the rabbis may go in order to avoid paying the poll-tax:

Raba said: "A rabbinic scholar may declare, I will not pay the poll tax, for it is written: 'It shall not be lawful to impose *mindah*, *belo*, or *halak* upon them.'"[30]   R. Judah then said: "*mindah* is the King's portion [of the crops]; *belo* is a head tax; and *halak* is *arnona* [possibly a produce tax, or a tax for the sustenance of marching troops]." Raba also said: "A rabbinical scholar may assert, 'I am a servant of fire, and will not pay poll-tax.'"[31]

The Persian government granted tax-exemptions to clergy in the Persian fire-cult. Therefore, Raba permitted rabbis to claim that they were fire-worshippers in order to avoid paying taxes![32] Of course, a rabbi would avoid the apparent heresy of claiming to be a fire-worshipper by thinking about the Lord as the "all consuming fire."[33]

The Talmud[34] presents laws and customs dealing with the business issues of local monopolies and restraint of trade. The discussion therein established the principles that scholars were exempt from certain business prohibitions. It also confirmed the right of a community to reserve a special space in the market for a worthy scholar:

Rabbi Dimi from Nehardea brought a load of figs in a boat. The Exilarch said to Raba, "Go and see if he is a scholar, and if so, reserve the market for him."[35]

Obviously, tax-exemptions and business advantages were desirable privileges that benefitted the early rabbinate. It is surprising that we do not find strong arguments against these benefits. Perhaps even those who opposed rabbinic benefits agreed that rabbis deserved the priestly prerogatives.[36]

C) Rabbinic salaries and fees

Let us now examine a tradition that is preserved in the

33

Talmuds of both Babylonia and *Eretz Yisrael* which provides evidence that, at least in certain places, it was acceptable to pay salaries to the teachers of Scripture. In the following passage the Gemara examines some of the consequences which result when one vows not to derive benefit from another:

"He may teach him *Midrash, Halakhot* and *Aggadot,* but not Scripture. Why not Scripture? Because it benefits him. But Midrash does not benefit him? Samuel said: 'This refers to a place where the teaching of Scripture is remunerated. But Midrash is not remunerated.' How state this definitely? The Tanna informs us that even where a fee is taken, it may be accepted only for Scripture and not for Midrash. Why does Midrash differ? Because it is written, 'And the Lord commanded me at that time to teach you.'[37] And it is also written, 'Behold I have taught you statutes and judgements even as the Lord my God has commanded me.'[38] Just as I taught you gratuitously, so you must teach gratuitously. Then should Scripture be remunerated? Rab said: 'The fee is for guarding the children.' Rabbi Johanan maintained: 'The fee is for teaching the accentuation.'"[39]

"It is written, "Behold, I have taught you statutes and ordinances.'[40] Just as I do so without remuneration, so you must do so without remuneration. Is it possible that the same rule applies [i.e., no remuneration] also to the teaching of Scripture and the translation? The text says, 'Statutes and ordinances.' Statutes and ordinances must be taught without remuneration, but not so Scripture and translation. And yet we see that those who teach Mishnah receive remuneration. Said Rabbi Judah b. Rabbi Ishmael, 'It is compensation for their loss of work.'"[41]

In the above passages one can sense the heightened tension between the "ideal" of scholars who "should" teach without compensation and the reality of the necessity of material support.

34

We see how the ideal (as reflected in the *d'rash* of Deut. 4.5, in B. Bekhorot 29a, that we should teach for free because God taught for free) is contradicted by the custom of some communities to pay fees to scholars. The contradiction is "resolved" by Rav and Rabbi Johanan who taught that the fees were compensation only for the *sekhar tirha* (i.e., the trouble and physical labor). The passage from the Talmud of *Eretz Yisrael*[42] is especially interesting. The Jerusalem Talmud determined that remuneration for the teaching of Scripture and translation was not prohibited *d'oraita*, and, by implication, that teachers of Scripture could receive direct fees. Only "statutes and judgements" (i.e. Mishnah and *halakhot*) had to be taught gratuitously. Even so, teachers of Mishnah were eligible for compensation for loss of time (*agar bateilah*).

While compensation by means of *sekhar tirha* and *sekhar batalah* was widely accepted, we cannot speak of a "professional" rabbinate without evidence of salaries. Salaries paid to scholars out of communal funds would free the scholar from the necessity of a secular occupation and would make him regularly available to attend to the community's needs. The following passages establish the existence of communal funds through which rabbis and judges received salaries:

R Judah stated in the name of R. Assi: "Those who enact laws (*gozrei gezerot*) in Jerusalem received their salaries out of the Temple funds [at the rate of] ninety-nine *maneh*. If they were not satisfied, they were given an increase." They were not satisfied? Are we dealing with wicked men? The reading in fact is: "[If the amount was] not sufficient, an increase was granted to them even if they objected."[43]

Of course, drawing salaries from communal funds was controversial. Such support seemed contradictory to the above mentioned prohibitions against deriving benefit from the Torah. The following two passages present additional evidence of rabbis who "enriched" themselves through their rabbinic office and of communities who paid rabbis salaries. Note especially the wistful hope that rabbis should rank highest among their brethren in wealth!

"There once arrived at the *beit midrash* [a gift of] a bag of dinars. Rabbi Ammi came in first and acquired them. But how may he do such a thing? Is it not written, 'And they shall give,'[44] but he shall not take it himself? Perhaps Rabbi Ammi acquired them on behalf of the poor. Or, if you wish, you may say that in the case of an eminent person it is different. For it has been taught: 'And the priest that is highest among his brethren' implies that he shall be highest among his brethren in beauty, in wisdom, and in wealth. Others say, 'Where is it proved that if he does not possess any wealth, his brethren, the priests, shall make him great?' It is proved in the Scripture: 'And the priest that is highest [by reason of gifts] from his brethren.'[45]

"Rabbi Simeon b. Menasha taught: If you see that the towns have been destroyed in the Land of Israel, you should know that it is because the inhabitants did not pay the scribes and the teachers their due salary."[46]

Already by the third century the rabbis had established the *halakhic* justification for an economic support system.[47] Indeed, it certainly appears that the rabbinate, as portrayed in the Talmud, already embodied the main characteristics of a professional institution. In the Talmud we find *halakhic* principles by which rabbis would receive financial compensation (*tirha* and *sekhar batalah*). Rabbis were exempt from poll-taxes. Rabbis were granted advantages in the business world. And finally, rabbis were understood to be the inheritors of the priestly benefits which included support from communal funds and tithes.

It is also clear that this professionalization was controversial and violated a cherished "ideal" that, likewise, was preserved in the Talmud.

What was the rabbinic ideal? Talmudic passages suggest that sincerity and true conviction were absolute musts for the rabbi. Raba said: "Any scholar whose inside is not like his outside is no scholar....Woe unto the enemies of the scholars [i.e., those corrupted scholars] who occupy themselves with the Torah, but have no fear of heaven."[48] The ideal rabbi had to be thoroughly versed in all matters of the halakhah. Rabbi Johanan said: "Who is the scholar that is appointed a leader of the community? He who when asked a matter of halakhah in any place can answer it, even in the Tractate Kallah."[49] The "ideal rabbi" supported himself by means of a secular vocation. Shammai was a builder; Rabbi Joshua was a blacksmith; Rabbi Jose was a tanner; Abba Hoshaiah of Turya was a laundryman; Rabbi Hanina and Rabbi Oshaya were shoemakers; Karna was a wine expert; Hisda and Rabbi Pappa were brewers of mead; and while other rabbis were sandal makers, carpenters and merchants, most worked in agriculture.[50] Thus, the ideal rabbi was a pious and humble man who sought no advantage due to his scholarship. He was thoroughly expert in all the law, and he supported himself by means of a secular vocation and devoted all his spare time to teaching and study. Is it any wonder, therefore, that many were unable to live up to the Talmud's rabbinic ideal?[51] It is in this vein that we can fully appreciate Rabbi Simeon b. Yochai's lament: "Is it possible? If a man ploughs in the ploughing season, and sows in the sowing season, and reaps in the reaping season, and threshes in the threshing season, and winnows in the season of wind, what is to become of the Torah?"[52]

How can we explain the contradictory traditions? One could make a case for the fact that the ideals of "gentlemen scholars" who refused to use their expertise for personal support and gain were ascribed to the early generations of Hillel and R. Tarfon respectively.[53] While the more permissive traditions were ascribed to the later Amoraic generations of Rab Judah and Raba.[54] But modern scholars are usually hesitant to put undue emphasis on the Talmudic attributions to specific personalities. Another explanation of the varying traditions is that the social realities changed and therefore Jewish custom was forced to adjust. This is certainly possible, but in which direction did the custom adjust? Must the ideal precede pragmatism?

The answer is beyond us. Still, it is enough that we recognize that even though there were varying opinions, the rabbinate of the first centuries of the common era was or was in the process of becoming a professional class. A significant number of rabbis saw themselves as the inheritors of priestly benefits. And like the priests, provision had to be made for the rabbi's material support and welfare. Incidentally, just from the Talmudic evidence we can see that the "common knowledge" (which maintains that the professional rabbinate was a creation of the 14th century) is, to say the least, an exaggeration.

As it turned out, the later *halakhic* authorities were generally permissive of rabbinic compensation, benefits and salaries. Some openly promoted the professionalization of the rabbinate, while others simply turned a blind eye to the fact that rabbis were being hired by communities.[55] Joseph Karo summarized the need for leniency in regard to rabbinic financial support:

"If there had not been support for those who study and teach on a regular basis, then no one would have been able to endure the hardship of Torah [study] as it is deserving [to be studied]."[56]

Yet, there was one great *halakhic* authority who was opposed to the professionalization of the rabbinate: Rabbi Moses Maimonides, the Rambam.

THE PROFESSIONAL RABBINATE AND MOSES MAIMONIDES

We divided rabbinic remuneration and benefits into three categories: a) compensation for "time and trouble;" b) tax-exemptions and business advantages; and c) salaries from communal funds. While Moses Maimonides (1135-1204) protested vigorously against the practice of rabbinic salaries, he approved the other forms of compensation and benefits. He wrote passionately against rabbinic salaries in both his commentary to the Mishnah (specifically, Mishnah *Avot* IV.5) and in his *halakhic* masterpiece, the *Mishneh Torah*. Let us begin by focusing on a few key passages in his lengthy commentary.

Rambam's commentary on Mishnah Avot IV.5 [57]

"After I had decided not to discuss this commandment, for it is quite clear, and since I also know that what I have to say on it does not please the majority of the great Torah scholars, or possibly all of them, I subsequently changed my mind concerning this decision, and I shall discuss it without considering earlier or contemporary works. Know that the meaning of the saying that "one should not make the Torah a spade with which to dig" is that one should not consider it a means for making a living. He [Hillel] explains and says that whoever benefits in this world from the honor of the Torah removes his life from the world (this is interpreted as "the World to Come"). People have misunderstood this clear expression, and have cast it aside in their mimicry of the nations, and have rather depended on literary meanings which they did not understand, as I shall explain. Thus, they imposed laws on individuals and on communities and caused people to think, in complete foolishness, that it was their logical and moral duty to support scholars and students, as well as men whose exclusive occupation is the study of the Torah. All this is a mistake. Neither in the Torah, nor in the words of the sages, is there any word that proves it true, nor a support on which they might lean at all...."

There are several interesting aspects to Rambam's commentary to Mishnah *Avot* IV.5. One is struck by Rambam's admission that most of the other *halakhic* authorities ("possibly all of them") disagreed with his position. Thus, by Maimonides' own account, most rabbinic authorities permitted scholars to receive salaries from the communal fund.[58] Of course, Rambam maintained that the other authorities all were mistaken, that they misunderstood the Talmud, and that some of them were "*hameshuga'im hamvohalim*," "confused fools."[59]

What is most evident is Rambam's opposition to rabbinical salaries from communal funds. And yet he was relatively lenient vis-a-vis the other categories of rabbinic benefits and compensation (*sekhar batalah*).

Maimonides agreed that rabbis qualified (*d'oraita*) for business advantages and tax exemptions. This was made clear in his commentary:

"On the other hand, what the Torah has permitted scholars to do is to give their money to someone to use it in business for them at his discretion, and that all the profit should be theirs, if he so agrees, and the one who does that for them has a great merit. A similar (permissible) practice is to give scholars merchandise in commission (so that they gain a profit), and to let them sell their merchandise first, at the opening of the market. These benefits God has decreed for them just as He has instituted the special gifts for the *kohen* and the tithe for the *levi*. Merchants even practice such customs as courtesies to each other, although no scholarship is involved. It is certainly in order that a scholar should be equal to a respected layman.

The Torah has exempted Torah scholars from special tributes as well as individual taxes. The community will exempt them from "head-taxes," and they [scholars] are relieved of building [fortification] walls and the like. Even if the Torah scholar happens to be a well-to-do man, he is free from any of the aforementioned obligations....This is a law of the Torah. Just as Torah freed the Temple priests from paying the half-shekel [so, too, are the rabbis exempt], as we have explained."[60]

In the same commentary, Maimonides also confirmed the legitimacy of compensation for loss and trouble (*sekhar batalah* and *tirha*):

"Karna was a judge. He would say, 'Give me someone to draw water in my place, or compensate me for my actual loss ("*batalti*"), and I will judge your case.'"

Still, Rambam was explicit in his disdain for those scholars who relied on public assistance. He wrote:

"One should strive not to be dependent on other people and not to be a public charge. So, too, the sages have enjoined us, saying: 'Rather make your Sabbath a weekday than be dependent on men.'[61] If reduced to poverty, even a distinguished scholar must not disdain manual labor, no matter how repulsive it is to him, in order to avoid dependence on others. One should preferably flay animal carcasses instead of telling the people: 'I am a great scholar, I am a priest, provide for me.' The sages have indeed commanded us to act like this. Some of the great sages derived their livelihood from chopping wood, carrying lumber, watering gardens, working in iron or making charcoal, and asked no help of the community; neither would they have accepted

41

charity had it been offered them."[62]

Rambam reiterated his opposition to communal support for Rabbis:[63]

"Anyone, however, who makes up his mind to study Torah and not work but live on charity (*tzedaqah*), profanes the name of God, brings the Torah into contempt, extinguishes the light of religion, brings evil upon himself and deprives himself of life hereafter. For it is forbidden to derive any temporal advantage from the words of the Torah. The sages said: 'Whoever derives a profit from use of the teachings of the Torah is helping to remove his life from the world.'[64] They have further charged us:

'Do not make it [the Torah] a crown by which to magnify yourself, nor a spade with which to dig.'[65] They, likewise, exhorted us: 'Love work, hate lordship.'[66] 'All study of the Torah, not conjoined with work, must, in the end, be futile and become a cause of sin."[67] The end of such a person will be that he will rob his fellow men."

Rambam's intention was that rabbis must support themselves by their 'worldly occupation.' Their free time must be devoted to the study of Torah. Maimonides disapproved of those who received charity in order to devote themselves solely to the study of Torah. Furthermore, he warned against spending too much time in "worldly occupations," lest the study of Torah be neglected. Thus, it appeared that Rambam offered Torah scholars two options: either be independently wealthy, or mortify yourself. Indeed, he championed the life of mortification in the next passage:

"The words of the Torah do not abide with one who studies listlessly, nor with those who learn amidst luxury and high living, but only with one who mortifies himself for the sake of the Torah, constantly enduring physical discomfort, and not permitting sleep

42

to his eyes or slumber to his eyelids...."[68]

Rambam maintained that manual labor was a virtue, even for Torah scholars. He referred to the example of Rav Joseph who carried heavy loads of wood, and he praised those who sweated from difficult labor. However, he did say: "As soon as the judge (*dayyan*) is appointed as the leader of the community, he must not do menial labor in front of three men (i.e., in public), so that he does not degrade himself in front of them."[69]

In any case, Rambam believed that the Jewish community of the future would not have to (or at least, *should not* have to) suffer the indignity of scholars and judges who receive salaries from communal funds. Ultimately, he said, God would provide for the scholars for doing the Lord's work.[70]

While the practice of rabbinic support from communal funds was contradictory to Rambam's ideal, Rambam also opposed the professional rabbinate because he saw it in the corrupting influence of the Babylonian *Gaonate*. Rambam identified the *Gaonate* as one of the great causes of the phenomenon of "rabbis for hire."[71] Isadore Twersky pointed out that Rambam chafed at the anachronistic *Gaonate* which relied upon pomp and circumstance and insisted on the formal retention of institutional prestige and primacy.[72] In fact, Rambam refused to grant the academies of Babylon sole right to the title "*Gaon*" (lit. "the pride" i.e., of Jacob). In his introduction to the *Mishneh Torah*, he conferred the title on sages everywhere:

"The sages, however, who arose after the compilation of the Talmud, studied it deeply and became famous for their wisdom, are called 'Gaonim.' These *Gaonim*, who flourished in the Land of Israel, Babylon, Spain and France, taught the method of the Talmud."

43

Twersky summed up Rambam's daring effort to wrest the primacy of the Babylonian *Gaonate*, saying:

> "Maimonides' *halakhic*-historical formulations underscored a basic socio-political fact: *Gaonic* teachings lacked intrinsic authoritativeness and could not possibly aspire to universal recognition. In other words, while the *Gaonim* constructed their platform upon a three-pronged supremacy--of the Oral Law, of the Babylonian Talmud, and of the Babylonian *Gaonim* in all matters of interpretation and application--Maimonides knocked out the third prong. Simultaneously, fully conscious of the fact that his forthright criticism would be uncongenial to most scholars, he repudiated the hierarchic-dynastic structure of the *Gaonate* and denounced their managerial methods, i.e., the maintenance of a retinue of scholars at public expense by relentless importuning for contributions. Oblivious of predecessors or contemporaries, he challenged the conventional proofs and values on which the system rested. The existence of an institutionalized and professionalized class of scholars supported by public and often high-pressured philanthropy was antithetical to Maimonides' existential posture as well as ideological position."[73]

Twersky's theory helps us understand that Rambam's battle to help create the ideal Jewish community forced him to take on the hierarchical status quo of the *Gaonate* and the image of the "professional rabbinate" which they promoted.

As Maimonides himself stated, the vast majority of the *halakhic* authorities had already decided in favor of rabbinic support from communal funds. Still, Rambam's opinion carried so much weight that 250 years later Rabbi Simeon ben Zemah Duran, in his defense of the professional rabbinate, was forced to say:

"I have seen that many people are grumbling at the fact that it was our custom throughout all the Jewish communities and many generations to give a salary to our scholars...they (who complain) base their argument in the light of what was written by the Rambam."[74]

Joseph Karo opposed Rambam's opinion on the professional rabbinate. Karo summarized the reasons for rabbinic salaries in his *Kesef Mishneh*. We will review Karo's analysis of the issue before drawing our final conclusions.

THE PROFESSIONAL RABBINATE AS EVIDENCED IN JOSEPH KARO'S KESEF MISHNEH

The *Kesef Mishneh*, by Joseph Karo (1488-1575), is an important commentary to Rambam's *Mishneh Torah*. As we review the *Kesef Mishneh to Hilkhot Talmud Torah* 3.10, note that Karo focused primarily on Rambam's earlier commentary to Mishnah *Avot* IV.5. Karo began:

"In his comments to Mishnah *Avot* IV.5, our Rabbi (Rambam) derides the support given to students and rabbis. [However,] it appears from his own comments that most of the great Torah scholars of his day, or even all of them, did [receive support from their communities]".[75]

Karo proceeded to systematically analyze Rambam's opposition to salaried rabbis. First, Karo dismissed Rambam's Talmudic examples of sages who supported themselves with their occupations and not from their rabbinical positions:

"He (Rambam) brings the example of Hillel the Elder[76] who was both a wood chopper and still studied. But there is no proof from this example, for this was, of course, at the beginning of his studies and it was during a time when there were thousands of students. Perhaps they only gave aid to some of them or, perhaps, anyone who could [support] himself would not receive benefits. But when a sage became worthy and he taught his wisdom to the people, he would be elevated accordingly. You should not think that he remained a wood chopper"!

Karo maintained that Rambam's opposition to rabbis who accepted charity and gifts was untenable in the light of Talmudic precedent. As Karo noted, the Talmudic sages taught that when one brought a gift to a scholar it was considered as if that person fulfilled the *mitzvah* of bringing the first-fruits to the Temple priests.[77] Karo also cited the example of the *dayyanei gezerot*[78] who received gifts and fees; and he pointed to the prophet Elisha[79] who received gifts and support. Karo continued his assault on Rambam's position by citing the example in the Talmud,[80] where once a gift of a bag of golden dinars arrived at the *beit midrash*. Rabbi Ammi came in first and took the gold. Karo paraphrased the text and then concluded:

"And there was no difficulty for them [those that protested] as to why he (Rabbi Ammi) took [the gift], except for the fact that he took it for himself. So, if it were not like this it would be correct [for him to take the gift]. Furthermore, as it is implied in the commentary, an eminent person, even if he takes the gift for himself, it is permitted."

Karo referred to the Tosafot in order to support his argument permitting rabbinic salaries:

"It says that scholars who taught the priests the laws of ritual slaughter and *kemitzah* [i.e., taking of a "handful" from the meal offering] received their salaries from the Temple funds.[81]

The *Tosafot* wrote that even though it is said in *Nedarim* that remuneration for study is forbidden, this case is different, for these [scholars] sit [and teach] all day and they do not have time to engage in any secular occupation. Since they have no other way to support themselves they take [remuneration] from the public. The words [of the *Tosafot*] teach us that salaries are not forbidden to those who teach except when they have other places from whence they might support themselves."[82]

In the above commentary, Karo restated the time honored *halakhic* tradition that the prohibition against rabbinic salaries was only valid when the rabbi was not full-time and could support himself in some other manner. In his conclusion to Rambam's Mishnah *Avot* commentary and *Hilkhot Talmud Torah* 3.10, Karo outlined the established guiding *halakhic* principles for the justification of the professional rabbinate:

"The general rule of the above is that any [scholar] who does not have enough for his support is permitted to take a salary from the public [funds] in order to decide cases or [receive remuneration] from the litigants....It is possible to say that the intention of our Rabbi [Rambam] here was that no man should cast off the yoke of a [secular] occupation and support himself from his fellow creatures just so he may study. But that one should learn a craft that will support him, and if he has enough, fine, but if he does not have enough, then he can receive support from the public. And this is basically what he [Rambam] wrote. He brought some Mishnaic passages which teach about the propriety of learning a craft. And even so, this is only the opinion of our Rabbi [Rambam] as it appears in his commentary to the Mishnah. In any event, we hold that when the *halakhah* is *rofefet beyadekha* (i.e., when the *halakhah* is unclear),[83] then follow after the popular custom (*minhag*). And we see all the sages of Israel before the time of our Rabbi [Rambam] and after him practiced the *minhag* of taking their salaries from the public. And also, even if one maintains that the

47

halakhah is according to the words of our Rabbi [Rambam] in his commentary to the Mishnah, then it is still possible to agree with all the sages of the generations [by recognizing that the sages simply followed the principle of]: 'It is time to act for the Lord; they have made void Your Torah;'[84] i.e., current necessity knows no law. In other words, if there had not been support for those who study and teach, then no one would have been able to endure the hardship of Torah [study] as it is deserving [to be studied]. And the Torah would have been forgotten, God forbid!

In his concluding comments, Joseph Karo made three important points. First, Karo implied that Rambam's opposition to rabbinic salaries was restricted to those defined in his commentaries. Was Karo insinuating that Rambam did not actively oppose rabbinical salaries in "the real world?" Was he suggesting that the *Mishneh Torah* was merely a theoretical work which only reflected Rambam's ideal? Perhaps. In his second point, Karo noted that, at the very least, the *halakhah* concerning the propriety of rabbinic salaries is unclear (*rofefet beyadekha*). When an issue is unclear, we follow popular custom (*minhag*), and the Talmudically documented custom was to support rabbis with financial compensation, benefits and salaries. Karo's third important point concluded that even if Rambam's ideal was *halakhically* correct (i.e., that rabbis should not be supported by communal salaries), the Jewish community could not survive the consequences of such a strict interpretation. Because the survival of the Jewish people was threatened, the sages had the right to violate even a Toraitic law in order to protect the integrity of Judaism and "build a fence around the whole Torah."[85]

The driving force behind Karo's entire argument, was that full-time professional rabbis were essential if Judaism was to continue to overcome the incessant challenges to its survival. It was quite apparent, even to the Talmudic sages, that it was incumbent upon the Jewish community to support the rabbinate.

In an ideal world, the people of Israel would all be well versed in Torah and would only turn to the rabbis for the most difficult issues. In the best of all possible worlds, scholars would have easy, well paying jobs which would enable them to devote ample time to their studies. There would be no need for them to receive public remuneration. Alas, as Karo realized, there was a gap between the ethical ideal and our moral responsibility. Therefore: *Et laasot la-adonai heferu toratekha* ("It is time to act for the Lord; they have voided Your Torah").[86]

CONCLUSION

Those of us who are interested in Progressive *halakhah* should take note of the courageous way the *halakhic* authorities addressed the tension between the "ethical ideal" and the moral necessity. The sages preserved the ideal of a rabbinate that was not reduced to mere occupation, and yet they realized that rabbis required financial support and benefits in order to serve the Jewish community. Idealists, like Rambam, opposed the professional rabbinate, but, by his own admission, he stood alone. Other authorities permitted salaries and benefits on two grounds. First, they believed that the Talmudic sources supported rabbinic compensation, benefits and even salaries from communal funds. Second, the *halakhic* authorities reasoned that even if the Talmudic "ideal" opposed the professional rabbinate, the *halakhah* would have to be changed out of practical necessity, because, as Joseph Karo asserted, the sages were charged with the moral responsibility of preserving the community. Sometimes, in order to fulfill that responsibility, we are called upon to overturn the *halakhah*: "It is time to act for the Lord; they have made void Your Torah."

The courage and sensitivity displayed by the sages in dealing with this vexing issue should serve as a model for all who wish to apply the traditions and ideals of our ancestors to the modern world.

RICHARD RHEINS

Notes

1. For example, cf. *Encyclopedia Judaica*, "Rabbi, Rabbinate," written by the editors, vol. XIII, pp. 1446-1447. "The office of rabbi was originally an honorary one on the principle that the Torah had to be taught free of charge. It was not until the 14th century that there is the first clear evidence of a rabbi receiving emoluments." The reference is to Rabbi Simeon ben Zemah Duran (Rashbaz). The Rashbaz, however, maintained that he was not the first professional rabbi and that "it was our custom throughout all Jewish communities and many generations to give a salary to oúr scholars". (Responsum #142). He traces The *halakhic* support for the professional rabbinate to the Talmud. Also, see the responsum by Solomon Freehof, *American Reform Responsa*, ed. Walter Jacob, New York, 1983, pp. 523-527.

2. Ephraim Urbach, *The Sages*, Cambridge, 1987, p. 601.

3. The title "rabbi" was not used by the earliest Jewish sages. Originally, it was accorded only to those who had received *semikhah*. The Babylonian scholars used the term "Rav." Since a rabbi was called upon to decide ritual and monetary cases he was also given the title *"Dayyan"* (i.e., "Judge"). Sephardic Jews used the title *"Hakham"* ("Sage") instead of "rabbi."

For a good review of the various titles used by Jewish scholars see *The Jewish Encyclopedia* ("Rabbi," p. 294), which also provides the text of Sherira Gaon's letter to Jacob ben Nissim with regard to the various titles that were used in different times and areas.

In order to avoid confusion, I will use the term "rabbi" in reference to both Sephardic and Ashkenazic scholars. Not infrequently, I will refer to rabbis simply as scholars. It is important to note that, for the most part, the various terms are interchangeably used throughout the rabbinic literature.

4. There are some scholars who have stricter definitions of the professional rabbinate. Dr. Irving Agus, for example, defines the professional rabbinate as involving these major issues: 1) payment and privileges; 2) unquestioned authority in his locality (i.e., the community would only address questions to their rabbi, the *"Rav ha-ir"*); and 3) exclusive authority in his locality (i.e., no other rabbi could come and contradict his rulings). See, I. Agus, *Urban Civilization in Pre-Crusade Europe*, New York, 1965, volume II, pp. 486-488. Of course, Agus' definition is much too narrow; it fits only the exception and not the normative realities of the rabbinate.

5. The translations in this paper are based on the Soncino editions. Words in brackets are my own explanatory notes. Words in parenthesis provide the English or Hebrew equivalent of the previous word.

6. See Mishnah *Avot* IV.5 (Albeck edition) for Rabbi Zadok and Hillel's opposition to those who "make worldly use of the Torah." Rabbi Tarfon (a third generation *Tanna*) was opposed to deriving any benefit whatsoever from his rabbinic position (B. Nedarim 62a).

7. See B. Ketubot 105a: "Rab Judah stated in the name of Rabbi Assi." B. Nedarim 62a, preserves Raba's support for rabbinic benefits.

8. M. *Avot* IV.5, and B. Berakhot 29a..

9. Mishnah *Avot* IV.5, quoted in full below, is listed as IV.7, in some editions. My reference is to Albeck's edition of the Mishnah.

10. "To sprinkle" refers to the ritual of purification of water mixed with the ashes of the Red Heifer. See Numbers 19:1-22, and Mishnah *Parah*.

11. M. Bekhorot IV.6.

12. Deuteronomy 4.5.

13. B. Bekhorot 29a.

14. Cf. Rambam's commentary to Mishnah *Avot* I.13.

15. Rabbah b. R. Shila, Ketubot 105b.

16. Nedarim 62a.

17. B. Bekhorot 29a.

18. Exodus 23.8.

19. B. Bekhorot 29a, and B. Qiddushin 56b.

20. B. Ketubot 105a.

21. M. Bekhorot IV.5.

22. B. Bekhorot 28b-29a.

23. This concept of compensation for *tirha* is further defined in B. Qiddushin 58b, where payment is acceptable in compensation for the physical act of bringing the ashes and drawing the water but no payment is permitted for sprinkling the waters, which is the actual act of sanctification.

24. B. Nedarim 62b.

25. *Ibid.*, 62a-62b.

26. J.T. Ma'aser Sheni 5.5, 56b; Lee I. Levine, *The Rabbinic Class of Roman Palestine in Late Antiquity*, Jerusalem, 1989, p. 71.

27. This is made clear in *Hagahot HaBah*, note #7.

28. Leviticus 21.8; B. Nedarim 62a.

29. B. Baba Batra 8a.

30. Ezra 7.24.

31. B. Nedarim 62b.

32. Shapur II tried to promote the Persian religion of fire worship by offering tax-exemptions. For a more comprehensive study of this phenomenon, see I. Epstein, in the Soncino edition of the Talmud (note #11 to Nedarim 62b), which refers to S. Funk, *Die Juden in Babylonien* II, p. 3.

33. Deuteronomy 4.24.

34. B. Baba Batra 22a.

35. *Ibid.*, 22a.

36. See Lee I. Levine, *The Rabbinic Class of Roman Palestine in Late Antiquity*, p.71.

37. Deuteronomy 4.14.

38. *Ibid.*, 4.5.

39. B. Nedarim 36b-37a.

40. Deuteronomy 4.5.

41. J.T. Nedarim 4.3.

42. *Ibid.*, 4.3.

43. B. Ketubot 105a. The *gozrei gezerot* (those who enacted *gezerot*) and the *dayyanei gezerot* (the *gezerah* judges) are both mentioned in this important passage. The fact that judges received a salary has stirred academic speculation. Ephraim Urbach in *The Halakhah, Its Sources and Development* (Massada, 1986, pp. 72ff.) maintains that the *gezerah* judges "were appointed in order to preserve traditions (ancient *gezerot* and court verdicts) and therefore they drew their salaries from the *shekel*-chamber...." others feel that this was done to permit the judges to serve on a full-time basis.

44. Deuteronomy 18.3.

45. B. Hullin 13b; cf. B. Yoma 18a, and B. Horayot 9a.

46. J.T. Hagigah 1.7.

47. See Lee I. Levine, *The Rabbinic Class of Roman Palestine in Late Antiquity*, pp. 69-71.

48. B. Yoma 72b.

49. B. Shabbat 114a. Rashi states that this requirement includes even the difficult tractate *Kallah*.

50. Judah David Eisenstein, "Rabbi," *The Jewish Encyclopedia*, pp. 294-295, Vol. X, pp 294-295.

51. See Ephraim Urbach, *The Sages*, London, 1987, pp. 601-608. "...The problem of the livelihood of the Sages in the framework of the question of studying Torah and practicing a craft did not cease troubling, complicating, and confusing the circles of the Sages" (p. 608).

52. B. Berakhot 35b.

53. Hillel lived during the last century B.C.E., and Rabbi Tarfon was a third generation Tanna (early second century of the Common Era).

54. Rab Judah was the second generation Amora (3-4 century C.E.) and Raba was a third generation Amora (4th century C.E.).

55. Rabbenu Gershom (960-1040) and R. Isaac Alfasi (1013-1105) both have references in their responsa to rabbis who were paid salaries yet they made no protest. Alfasi (Responsum #223) dealt directly with the issue of a rabbi's contracted salary with a community. He supported the rabbi. Also, see the important responsa and commentaries of Rabbi Simeon Ben Zemach Duran. Duran erroneously is referred to as the "first professional rabbi." His comments trace the *halakhic* principles from the Talmud through the later authorities for support of professional rabbinate. Translations of Duran include: Isidore Epstein, *The Responsa of Rabbi Simon B. Zemah Duran*, New York, 1930; and Solomon Freehof, *A Treasury of Responsa*, Philadelphia, 1963, pp.79-80.

56. *Kesef Mishneh* commentary to Rambam's *Mishneh Torah, Hilkhot Talmud Torah*, 3.10.

57. For a complete translation to Rambam's commentary to Mishnah *Avot*, see Paul Forchheimer, *Maimonides' Commentary of Pirkey Avot*, New York, 1983. Forchheimer's edition of Mishnah *Avot* lists the passage under review as *Avot* IV.7. My reference is to the Hebrew text of Rambam's commentary printed in the Babylonian Talmud by the Gross Brothers, Printing Co. Inc., Union City, NJ. There, Rambam's commentary is ascribed to *Avot* IV.5.

58. Note that Rambam acknowledged that most of the *halakhic* authorities permitted rabbis to receive salaries. This establishes the existence of a communal-professional rabbinate a full 250 years before R. Simeon b. Zemach Duran ("the first professional rabbi").

59. Rambam makes this remark in the middle of his comments to *Avot* IV.5.

60. Mishnah *Avot* IV.5.

61. B. Shabbat 118a.

62. *Mishneh Torah, Zera'im* 10.18.

63. *Mishneh Torah, Talmud Torah* 3.10.

64. *Avot* IV.5.

65. *Ibid.*, IV.5.

66. *Ibid.*, I.10.

67. *Ibid.*, II.2.

68. *Mishneh Torah, Talmud Torah* 3.2.

69. *Ibid., Hilkot Shoftim* 25.4.

70. See *Mishneh Torah, Shemitah V'Yovel* 13.13.

71. Isadore Twersky, *Introduction to the Code of Maimonides (Mishneh Torah)*, New Haven, 1980, pp. 82-83.

72. *Ibid.*, pp. 82-83.

73. *Ibid.*, pp. 82-83.

74. Responsum #142. The translation is my own. Cf. Solomon Freehof's translation in *A Treasury of Responsa*, JPS, Philadelphia, 1963, pp. 79-80.

75. S.v. *"kol hamasim al libo;"* the translations of the *Kesef Mishneh* are my own.

76. B. Yoma 35b.

77. B. Ketubot 105b.

78. *Ibid.*, 105a.

79. II Kings 4.42.

80. B. Hullin 134b.

81. B. Ketubot 106a.

82. *Kesef Mishneh* to *Hilkot Talmud Torah* 3.10.

83. [When the law] "is flimsy in your hand" is a literal translation of "*rofefet be-yadekha*." This phrase comes from the Jerusalem Talmud Pe'ah 7.6: "Concerning any law that is unclear to the court, and you do not know what behavior to follow, observe how the community behaves and act similarly."

84. Psalms 119.126. "*Et laasot laadonai, heferu toratekha*" means, of course, that desperate times demand desperate actions. There is much discussion in the rabbinic literature concerning this verse and the principle it represents. The principle of "voiding the Torah in order to act for the sake of the Lord," is used by the rabbis to justify certain actions which may be performed in violation of expressed Toraitic law. Rashi, in his commentary to B. Berakhot 63a, brings forth one of the classic examples of this principle: "Those who do His will have violated His Torah, like Elijah on Mount Carmel, who sacrificed on a non-central altar during a period when that was forbidden, because it was a time to make a fence and a hedge among the Jews for the sake of the Holy one, blessed be He." See Joel Roth, *The Halakhic Process*, New York, 1986, pp. 169 ff.

85. See note #85 above. Karo was certainly aware that Rambam himself recognized the necessity of violating the strict reading of the Torah in order to protect the overall integrity of Judaism. See Rambam's *Mishneh Torah, Hilkhot Mamrim* 2.9.

86. Psalms 119.126.

ETHICAL IMPERATIVE AND HALAKHIC INNOVATION

Moshe Zemer

I. HILLEL THE ELDER - A SOLUTION FOR ILLEGITIMACY

An epidemic of *mamzerut* swept over the Jewish community of Alexandria around the first year of the Common Era. It was the custom of Alexandrian Jewish men to betroth their wives a year before a marriage (a practice not dissimilar to that in the Biblical period and among Yemenite Jews of recent generations). In this hiatus between *qiddushin* (betrothal) and *nessuin* (marriage), other Jewish men would often take these betrothed women as their wives. The sages of Alexandria were about to pronounce the children fathered by these "second husbands" as *mamzerim* (illegitimate). They relied on the established *halakhah* that a woman betrothed by *qiddushin*, is considered a married woman, her relationship with another man is adulterous and their issue *mamzerim*.

These troubled people turned to Hillel the Elder in *Eretz Yisrael* for help. He instructed representatives of the younger generation: "Bring me your mothers' *ketubot* (marriage contracts)."[1] At that time the *ketubah* was composed by laypeople and varied in its text from place to place. Hillel scrutinized the document and found the following: *lekheshetikansi lahuppah, hevi li leintu* - "when you enter the *huppah* (marriage canopy), be thou my wife."

Hillel the Elder took this phrase out of context and interpreted it as though it were a condition: Only when you enter the *huppah* will you be wife, but if you don't enter the *huppah* with me you are not betrothed. The result was that those women who did not reach the *huppah* with their fiances were proclaimed retroactively "unbetrothed." Therefore they were neither adulterous nor were their offspring blemished.[2]

By what means did Hillel succeed in making this radical transformation? The Talmud tells us that the great sage *haya doresh leshon hedyot* - he used to interpret common language, like that of the marriage contract written by a layperson, as if it were a rabbinic condition. Prof. Yitzhak Gilat of Bar Ilan University explains that Hillel gave *halakhic* approval to a lay custom; i.e., the text of the *ketubah*, and then used this custom as if it were a formula set by rabbinic sages.[3]

How could Hillel deal this way with a *mitzvah deoraita* - a Scriptural commandment regarding the forbidden status of a betrothed woman who, according to the *halakhah*, must be divorced before remarrying? The sages of Alexandria, who were determined to blemish the children, did indeed have the letter of the Law on their side.

It appears that Hillel, when confronted with the plight of these young people, felt compelled to use a legal fiction to save them from *mamzerut* (illegitimacy). The normative law stated that the children of a betrothed woman by another man are *mamzerim*, so his best course was to prove that she wasn't previously betrothed. We might well ask how Hillel the Elder, one of the framers of the *halakhah*, could have treated the law in such a fashion? Before trying to answer this question let us determine whether this was an isolated incident.

II. RABBAN GAMLIEL - TESTIMONY REFORM

Hillel's grandson, Rabban Gamliel the Elder, was confronted with the consequences of the massacre of Jews at Tel Arza. The unidentified bodies of innumerable Jewish men forewarned the danger that almost as many widows would be left *agunot* (chained). Valid testimony of a husband's death was required for the widow to remarry. The Torah established: "Only on the evidence of two witnesses, or of three witnesses, shall a matter be sustained,"[4] which was codified as *halakhah*. [5]

Nevertheless, Rabban Gamliel permitted these women to remarry on the basis of the hitherto invalid testimony of one witness (instead of the required two), hearsay evidence (*eid mipi eid*) or the testimony of a woman of a maidservant.[6]

Once again a Biblical injunction was circumvented; this time *edut p'sulah* (invalid testimony) was accepted to free unfortunate women from the chains of widowhood. We may ask the same question of Rabban Gamliel that was asked of his grandfather: How could the President of the Sanhedrin make such a drastic departure from the accepted laws of testimony? Hillel and Rabban Gamliel were confronted with problematic ethical situations for which there was no apparent solution in the accepted *halakhah pesukah* (authoritative law) of their time. They were unable to turn their backs on unfortunates who were punished for no fault of their own. They could not consider a non-*halakhic* or extra-*halakhic* solution. Therefore by means of interpretation, at times quite forced, or through the use of a *taqanah* (rabbinic decree), they resolved an intolerable injustice. Could this laudable action justify taking the *halakhah* into their own hands? Whence did they derive the authority to make these far reaching changes, which were so controversial?

When the rabbis met victims of oppression, they did not theorize about the unethical character of the latter's predicament. Armed with prophetic insight and rabbinic *pesaq* (legal decision) they felt a moral responsibility to take *halakhic* action to relieve their suffering.

61

Rabbi Eliezer Berkovits, professor emeritus of the orthodox Hebrew Theological College in Skokie, proclaims that "The rabbis in the Talmud were guided by the following insight: God forbid that there should be anything in the application of the Torah to the actual life situation that is contrary to the principles of ethics."[7] If a ruling is *halakhic*, it must be ethical. If it is unethical, it cannot be *halakhic*.

The Talmudic sages and later decisors witnessed many tragedies that were the effect of slavishly literal interpretations of the existing *halakhah*. When a proportion of the people felt they were suffering from unethical rulings, the existing legal approach lost its exclusive *halakhic* validity. Therefore by offering a different approach, even if it be a legal fiction, the moral problem might be resolved. This new approach then became part of the *halakhah*. Here we have *halakhic* innovations initiated by an ethical imperative and eventually becoming part of the ongoing *halakhic* system.

Not only in the authoritative Talmudic period did scholars allow themselves to innovate but also, as we shall see, in a decision that was rendered many centuries later.

III. RABBI MOSES ISSERLES - AN ORPHAN'S DIGNITY

Throughout the generations the sages initiated *halakhic* principles which enabled them to rule leniently and even permit the forbidden. One such principle established that in "a time of emergency,"[8] it is permissible to make a lenient decision and permit a rabbinic prohibition. The first generation Babylonian Amora, Rab, permitted carrying Hanukkah candles on Shabbat because this was an emergency situation. The candles must be hidden from the Parsees who ruled that it was forbidden for Jews to light them.[9]

The second principle is explicitly stated in the Talmud: "Great is human dignity because it overrides a negative prohibition in the Torah,"[10] namely the Scriptural command: "You shall not turn aside from the verdict which they declare to You."[11]

This latter verse serves as the authoritative source of rabbinical precepts. Nevertheless, in order to protect human dignity so that no person would be publicly deprecated, it was permitted to disobey a rabbinic prohibition.[12]

More than a millennium later, Rabbi Moses Isserles (Rama) of Krakow, Poland (1525?-1572), employed these Talmudic principles to resolve a difficult and urgent problem. In one of his responsa he relates the controversy over a dowry, which delayed the wedding of an orphan bride that was to take place on a Friday:

"When the shadows of evening began to fall and the Sabbath was approaching, her relatives who were to give the dowry closed their fists and refused to give a sufficient amount....Then the groom absolutely refused to marry her. He paid no attention to the pleas of the leaders of the city that he refrain from putting a daughter of Israel to shame for the sake of mere money....Then they finally agreed and the groom consented to enter under the *huppah* and no longer to shame a worthy daughter of Israel. Thereupon I arose and conducted the marriage at that hour."[13]

The timing of this wedding, as described by Isserles, was "in the dark of night on Friday evening, an hour and a half after night had fallen."[14]

The Rama found it necessary to justify his action on the Sabbath, because some of the outstanding members of the Krakow community had lodged complaints. His vindication included the two above mentioned Talmudic principles.

a. It is possible to permit a wedding after the beginning of the Sabbath since it was a time *of emergency,* because "the maiden would have been put to shame if she had to wait for the wedding until the end of the Shabbat after she had already immersed herself." In this difficult situation Isserles relied on Rabbenu Tam who stated that the Rabbinic sages permitted one to betroth a woman on the Shabbat when it was a matter of great distress.[15] Isserles interpreted his ruling to mean:

"It is clear that, in a great emergency, we may permit such a marriage. There can be no greater emergency that this case in which a grown orphan girl was being put to shame. It would be a lifelong disgrace for her, enough to set her apart from all other girls."

b. His action was also justified by the principle of human dignity:

"Great indeed is the commandment to be considerate of the honor due human beings. It sets aside the negative commandment...in this case it is only a rabbinic prohibition...besides our concern that the match might be broken and there might be no marriage at all as a result of quarreling between the families. ' Great is the value of peace between man and wife! ' "[16]

Isserles shows that these two principles provide the moral infrastructure for a Talmudic *pesaq* (ruling) dealing with many *halakhic* questions. His concern for the unfortunate bride led him to officiate at her wedding in spite of *halakhic* prohibitions and the opposition of the elders of the Kracow Jewish community. His *halakhic* decision was a matter of conscience, as indicated by the conclusion of his responsum:

"The truth is that the need of the hour leads us to be lenient in such matters which are only an additional prohibition of the rabbis. The rabbinical prohibitory decrees were not meant to apply in times of emergency...what can be done if the hour has moved along until darkness, and there is ground for concern that the match may be broken or the maiden put to shame? Under such circumstances, he who relies on the above arguments to be lenient has not done harm. May he enjoy in peace the joy of the Sabbath thereafter. The good deed that he has done will atone for him, if his intention was for the sake of Heaven and peace."

IV. RABBI MOSHE GALANTE - REDEMPTION OF A CHILDLESS WIDOW

In 1580 Rabbi Moshe Galante, a disciple of Rabbi Joseph Caro, succeeded his teacher as Rabbi of Safed. One of his most famous responsa deals with the case of a young childless widow who asked her brother-in-law (*yavam*) to give her *halitzah* (release from levirate marriage), but was refused. Apparently there was a great deal of property involved. For a period of two years since her husband's death, "a conflagration of fire was ignited between the two families. Every day a number of quarrels and arguments broke out between the family of the widow and the family of the brother-in-law who kept insisting on *yibbum* - (levirate marriage)."[17]

The questioner presents Rabbi Galante with the following narrative:

"Then one day the relatives of the widow were advised to instruct her to go to the synagogue in the community of her brother-in-law. At the time of the reading of the Torah she was to approach her brother-in-law and spit in his face. This is what happened. She came to the synagogue on a Monday at the time of the Torah reading, stood in front of her brother-in-law and spat in his face three times, and each time with spit that was apparently seen, in the presence of the entire congregation. Each time she said: 'This is the *yavam* that wants to take me in levirate marriage

65

- I don't want you!'"

She spat thrice while three members of the congregation testified that she passed before them and they made a *beit din* judgement as is inscribed there.

The questioner then concluded with a number of *halakhic* queries:

What is the status of the widow? Is she forbidden to her levir? Must she therefore be given *halitzah*? Is there power in this spitting to forbid her to her brother-in-law, so that he must give her *halitzah*?

The main point to clarify was whether this staged act of spitting in the synagogue, in the presence of three men who sit as a rump *beit din* (court), may give the widow the status of a *halutzah* (one who has received levirate release), which would have prevented her brother-in-law from taking her in levirate marriage. Can this partial "*halitzah*," without removal of a sandal, with no declaration by the *yavam* and without his consent be considered sufficient to make his sister-in-law forbidden to him?

Rabbi Galante replies in a long, closely argued responsum that the deed perpetrated in the synagogue cannot be construed as valid *halitzah*. Nevertheless, it has the power to eliminate the possibility of *yibbum*: "In this case there is no one who will claim that she may be taken in levirate marriage. Rather she must receive *halitzah*." The decisor thereby gives his *post factum* approval of the desparate staged act of the young woman, that blocked her brother-in-law from chaining her to him. Now he must give her *halitzah*.

One question remains: "It is important to know whether a *beit din* has the power to *force* the *yavam* (to give *halitzah)* or not?" It is clear that he must release her, but is it possible to compel him to do so? To this the Safed rabbi responds:

"Since she may not be taken in levirate marriage, we force (the levir) to release her through *halitzah*."

This great rabbi gave his *halakhic* imprimatur to the desparate and blatantly extra-*halakhic* act of the unfortunate woman and thereby untied her bonds.

V. RABBI JUDAH LEIB ZIRELSOHN - MARRIAGE OF A *KOHEN* AND A CONVERT

At the beginning of the twentieth century, Rabbi Yehudah Leib Zirelsohn of Kishinev wrote a remarkable responsum to a Bulgarian rabbi concerning a young woman who had converted to Judaism.[18] Two years after her conversion, she became engaged to a Jew in her city. After all the preparations for the wedding had been completed, it was discovered that the bridegroom was a *kohen* (of priestly descent) and therefore forbidden to marry a convert.

The bride's parents, who had willingly agreed to her conversion, belonged to one of the outstanding families of the city. Her family was now shocked at the refusal to allow her to marry her fiance. "The local Christian community was in an uproar over this flagrant insult to the family by treating their daughter like a prostitute." The bridegroom had threatened to convert to Christianity together with his fiance if they were not married by the rabbi. The Bulgarian rabbi asked for permission to marry them "in order to prevent a *hilul hashem* (desecration of God's Name) and especially at a time like this, when anti-Semitism is so rampant."

Rabbi Zirelsohn, the leader of Agudat Yisrael in Bessarabia, wrote a learned *halakhic* responsum to this query. He contrasted the prohibition of an individual couple, a *kohen* and a convert with *mitzvah d'rabim* (the *mitzvah* of general welfare) of the Jewish community which must be saved from a possible pogrom. Zirelsohn further linked the prohibition of this marriage with the anticipated danger that these young people might become apostates and, therefore, proclaimed:

"Most surely we must dismiss the interdictions of the marriage of a *kohen* with a convert for this couple which is on the brink of an abyss...in order to save them from an incessant betrayal of the entire Torah by these two souls angrily leaving the religion of Israel."

In conclusion, Rabbi Zirelsohn gave the Bulgarian rabbi an *halakhic* judgement which allowed him to marry the couple, on condition that he widely publicize that this step does not constitute a precedent and that he notify the *hatan* (bridegroom) that he and his offspring are disqualified as *kohanim*.

We have studied five great decisors whose services to Israel stretch over a period of two millenia. With what qualifications were these scholars invested that enabled them to respond to the suffering of their people and to resolve their problems?

These rabbis and many others like them became great moral authorities because they acquired or were blessed with at least four traits:

1) A commanding knowledge of the tradition
2) Sensitivity to the suffering of individuals
3) The desire and determination to help
4) The courage to decide and to carry out their decision.

Therefore the plight of *mamzerim*, *agunot* or a couple prevented from marrying was perceived by the rabbis as an ethical imperative which they must resolve. In view of the religious and legal framework in which they lived they were able to resolve the moral problems that confronted them only by *halakhic* innovations.

Finally, what was the source of their authority to make such radical changes? We may consider the two following answers:

One is a reported discussion between two Talmudic scholars debating the question how rabbinic sages could make decisions which seemingly conflicted with the accepted *halakhah*. One scholar said that they were able to make these innovative decisions, because they were *g'dolei haTorah* (great rabbinic authorities). No, retorted the other, they were *g'dolei haTorah* because they *made* such decisions.

Rabbi Moses Isserles gave the following justification for this authority in a responsum thats warrant one of his own radical *halakhic* innovations:

"When new circumstances develop that were unknown to ancient authorities and there is the fear of ruination or prohibition that was not suspected in ancient times, *it is certainly permitted to institute new enactments.*"[19]

Rabbis of every age were called upon to react with sensitivity to the ethical imperative of the suffering of their age. They instituted new enactments and *halakhic* innovations with the determination and courage to assuage the anguish of their distressed generation.[20]

MOSHE ZEMER

Notes

1. B. Baba Metziah 104a.

2. *Ibid.*, 104a.

3. Yitzchak Gilat, "The Relation of Halakhah to Reality," *Studies in Problems of Culture, Education and Society* (Hebrew),4, Tel Aviv, 1972, p. 72.

4. Deuteronomy 19.15.

5. *Mishneh Torah*, Hilkhot Edut 4.1.

6. M. Yevamot 16.7.

7. *Not in Heaven, The Nature and Function of Halakhah* (sub-section entitled: "*Halakhah* as the Priority of the Ethical"), New York: KTAV, 1983, p. 19. *Vide* my chapter "Authority and Criteria in Liberal *Halakhah*," in *Dynamic Jewish Law*, ed. Walter Jacob and Moshe Zemer, Tel Aviv and Pittsburgh, 1991, p. 14.

8. B. Shabbat 45a.

9. *Ibid.*, 45a. The Parsees, being fire worshippers, decreed that no one may light candles on their (the Parsees') festivals except in Parsee houses of worship. Fire was forbidden in the houses of Jews at such times. Since the Hanukkah *menorah* was lit near the street it would have to be hidden whenever a Parsee would approach.

10. B. Berakhot 19b. See Maimonides, *Sefer Hamitzvot*, Haim Heller edition, Jerusalem, 1980, Negative Precept, #312, p. 179.

11. Deuteronomy 17.11.

12. See Yitzchak Gilat, *op. cit.,* p. 206, footnote 2.

13. Moses Isserles, *Responsa Harama*, ed. Asher Ziv, Jerusalem, 1971, Responsum no. 128, pp. 488-495; The translation is based in part on Solomon B. Freehof, *A Treasury of Responsa*, Philadelphia, 1962, pp. 113-117. All further references to Isserles are from this source. See Rama's gloss to *Shulhan Arukh* Orah Hayyim 339.9, which was apparently written in the wake of the incident discussed in the responsum.

14. Freehof, *op.cit.*, p.114.

15. Rabbenu Tam's statement is quoted in Moses Coucy, *Sefer Mitzvot HaGadol*, Jerusalem, 1961, Negative Precepts, #71-75.

16. B. Hullin 141a.

17. *Responsa R. Moshe Galante*, Livorna, 1608, responsum, #80, pp. 45a-46b.

18. Judah Lieb Zirelsohn, *Responsa Ma'arkhei Lev*, Kishinev, 1930, Even Haezer, Resp. 72.

19. *Responsa HaRama, op. cit.,* Responsum #19, footnote 8, (Emphasis added).

20. *Vide* my article, "Halakhah as a Developmental and Moral Phenomenon" (Hebrew), *Shalhevet*, Jerusalem: Israel Movement for Progressive Judaism, September, 1987, #34, pp. 4ff; or in its French version, "Il est certainment permis de modifier toutes les decisions rabbiniques," *Tenoua*, Paris: MJLF, Decembre 1987, 47, pp. 3ff; Printemps, 1991, 58, pp. 19ff.

THE RABBI AS ARBITER

Peter Haas

There is a governing presumption in Jewish law that the *halakhah* has no gaps. The revelation given to Moses at Sinai covers every contingency, either directly or through analogy. For this reason, it is understood, the courts and judges who adjudicate disputes in Judaism do not in fact make law, as we seem to take for granted in the American judicial system. Rather it is the goal of the court and its judges to discover the proper precedent for the case at hand. Legislation is a matter of the Divine. What is left in human hands is merely the application.

It has become an unquestioned, widely accepted, and wrong assumption today that the only valid institution for such an adjudication of disputes within the Jewish community was the *beit din* and that all such decisions were to be made only by scholars. This assumption has been pushed, of course, by the Orthodox rabbinate in its attempt to delegitimize any attempt by non-Orthodox rabbis, scholars or laypeople to make any pronouncements whatsoever as regards what might count as proper Jewish practice. In fact another institution existed outside the *beit din*, an institution which was always given *halakhic* recognition. This institution is the arbitration court. I want to describe this little known institution of Jewish law, pointing out in the process that the *halakhah* until modern times was much more diverse, open and tolerant that the current Orthodox myth allows. The *halakhah*, the arbitration court shows, was hardly "orthodox" at all.

The origin of this legal mechanism, that is, arbitration, as a parallel to the formal *batei din*, is lost in the mists of history. The general consensus is that is has its roots in the Greco-Roman legal system.[1] In all events, it was already taken, more or less, for granted by the time the Mishnah was compiled. The fact the Tannaim saw the two types of courts as essentially equivalent. In either case the litigants come before a panel that elicits testimony from approved witnesses and then issues a ruling in line with accepted practice and custom. It thus comes as no surprise that the early rabbinic literature makes no distinction between setting up a *beit din* and setting up a court to handle an arbitration, since the two procedures are in fact identical. The identification of these two court systems in the minds of the Tannaim is clear from the Mishnah,[2] which discusses the makeup of the court, but which is also the *locus classicus* for the arbitration board. It describes the procedure as follows:

"Property cases are [decided by] three [judges]. 'This litigant chooses one [judge], and that litigant chooses one judge, and then the two of the [litigants] choose one more,' the words of R. Meir. And the sages say, 'The two judges choose one more.'"[3]

What we have here is a normal three-judge panel, of the type that adjudicates all civil disputes in Judaism. The arbitration is conceived as no different from any other court case. The only apparent difference is that an arbitration panel is not a sitting court, but is appointed by the litigants on an *ad hoc* basis. In this way the arbitration panel is different from the Sanhedrin which was presumably a permanent body made up of scholars.

The more informal nature of the arbitration panel raises immediately the practical question of how its members are to be chosen. Can anyone serve on such a panel or are there some qualifications or limitations? The Mishnah[4] seems to assume that anyone can serve if appointed. The question is addressed more directly in the same Mishnah, which describes the grounds for dismissing a proposed panel member:

"This party has the right to invalidate the judge chosen by that one, and that party has the right to invalidate the judge chosen by this one, the words of R. Meir. And sages say, 'Under what circumstances? When he brings evidence about them, that they are

74

relatives or [otherwise] invalid [to serve as judges]. But if they are valid [judges] or experts recognized by a court he does not have the power to invalidate them."[5]

The above dispute may seem trivial but in fact concerns a major conceptual difference between Meir and the sages over the nature of the arbitration panel. The point around which the dispute revolves becomes clear in light of the discussion presented in the Yerushalmi. The question is asked as to why Meir asserts that each litigant has the right to choose one of the judges. The answer, given in the name of R. Zira, is that "since the litigant chooses the judge, he takes for granted that his choice will seek cause in his own behalf."[6] Meir's idea, then, is that the judges are not so much meant to serve as a fact finding board as a panel of advocates. This view of law is much more familiar to us from the Anglo-American tradition, where, let us say, judges on the Supreme Court are simply assumed to hold certain positions and the appointment of one is a matter of public politics. The sages reject this theory, holding instead that the members of the panel are in fact like regular court judges; that is, neutral observers open only to the facts of the case. For this reason, a nominee may be excluded from serving on the arbitration panel only if he has a personal interest in the outcome, the same criterion that enters into the acceptance of witnesses. In other words, once a judge is deemed impartial he cannot be challenged on grounds of personal politics. What is also interesting in the case of an arbitration panel is that there is no requirement that the nominee be a recognized scholar. Any disinterested party may be nominated. I will return to the implications of this.

Although some of the rules of the formal beit din apply to the arbitration panel, it is also clear that the decision reached in arbitration need not be in conformity with the strict requirements of halakhah in order to be deemed valid. This is, I believe, of major significance. The arbitration panel is free to do as it deems

75

best, and its decision has formal *halakhic* recognition. A good example of the legal status of arbitration comes from the *Shulhan Arukh*, in connection with what we might call plea bargaining; that is, an argument to reach a solution before a formal verdict is rendered. The relevant passage from Hoshen Mishpat reads as follows:

"It is a *mitzvah* to say to the litigants at the start of the trial, 'Do you want a legal judgement or a compromise (*p'sharah*)?' If they want a compromise, they come to a compromise between them. And just as one is warned not to bias the law, so is one warned not to bias the compromise toward the one side over the other. And any court that always forges compromises is to be praised. When is this the case? Before all the evidence has been presented. Even if the judge has heard their arguments and knows which way the law inclines, it is still a *mitzvah* to execute a compromise. But after the evidence has been presented and the judge has said, 'So-and-so you are acquitted and so-and-so you are liable,' then they are not authorized to enter into a compromise between them."[7]

This passage throws some light on the legal status of a compromise. For once the evidence is formally known, then the force of formal law takes over. The judge can no longer allow a settlement or compromise. Before the trial has run its course, however, the litigants can agree to end the proceedings and come to a private agreement. This agreement will be outside the law, as it were. That is, it might be quite different from what the applicable legal paradigm would require. Nonetheless, the court is encouraged to effect such a compromise. And further, while the creation of a compromise is a way of avoiding the strict application of the law, it nonetheless has the force of *halakhah*, as the *Shulhan Arukh* goes on to make clear. The point is that the judge as arbiter in this case is acting in a very different capacity than he does when he formally announces a verdict after a completed trial.

76

What is interesting about such binding arbitration is that it was allowed to continue as a form of conflict resolution alongside, but distinct from, the formal institution of the *beit din*. The fact that arbitration panels were an alternative system of justice seems to have been already recognized in Roman times. Asher Gulak cites an example of a Roman law that recognizes the right of Jews in the empire to go to their own courts rather than Roman courts if they agree to arbitration. Presumably the sides would choose judges according to the pattern enunciated by the Mishnah and could reach a solution in this way outside the bounds of Roman law.[8] According to Gulak this type of court was generally recognized as having jurisdiction in the Jewish community even when in all other cases Jewish legal self-rule was restricted by the governing power. Thus the Roman recognition of arbitration as a legitimate alternative to formal court proceedings provided an important precedent for the future struggle to maintain Jewish institutional and legal autonomy. Although the subject has not been researched sufficiently, it seems that Jewish communities routinely resorted to such arbitration courts when outside powers restricted the jurisdiction of formal Jewish courts.[9] Thus some semblance of Jewish communal autonomy was retained. I want to investigate this phenomenon a bit more closely.

This resort to arbitration courts in order to get around imperial restrictions developed especially in post-Talmudic times. The basic structure of these panels was developed in Sassanian Babylonia; notwithstanding the fact that the Jewish community was generally allowed legal autonomy within the late Persian empire. The rabbis and gaonim of Babylonia knew of the Roman legal tradition and adopted it to their own needs. For the Babylonian masters, this sort of litigation, in which both parties agreed to a compromise, was deemed superior to the imposition of a legal ruling. On this we can cite, for example, the following Talmudic passage:

"R. Judah b. Korha says: Settlement by arbitration is a meritorious act, for it is written: 'Render judgement of truth and peace in your gates.'[10] Surely where there is strict justice there is no peace, and where there is no peace, there is no strict justice! But what is that kind of justice with which peace abides? -- We must say: arbitration."[11]

For the Babylonians, then, arbitration, rather than being a legal fiction for avoiding court trials, turns out to be a preferable mode of solving disputes. The reason is, of course, that both sides concur in the settlement and so will be willing to see matters through in good faith. In fact, I think it is fair to say that the framers of the Talmud not only preferred arbitration to full-blown legal action, but actually were prepared to say that arbitration had stronger legal warrants than an imposed settlement:

"R. Simeon b. Gamaliel says: Legal judgement is by three; arbitration is valid if made by two. And the force of arbitration is greater than that of legal judgement, for if two judges decide a case, the litigants can repudiate their decision, but if two judges arbitrate, the parties cannot repudiate their decision."[12]

Despite its possible origin as an extra-legal institution, then, it is clear that arbitration courts quickly became a recognized and even honored element of Jewish communal structure. As such, these courts continued to function throughout the Middle Ages. Gulak, for example, has collected number of "arbitration documents."[13] These give us a good idea of how the procedure worked. Responsa from the Middle Ages also indicate the procedure was given full legal recognition. At times, arbiters were deemed equivalent in all respects to regular judges.[14] A few differences did persist however. In some cases the case brought to arbitration had to be argued with 24 hours.[15] Rules of evidence could be much more relaxed than in a formal hearing and with few exceptions the arbiters did not have to issue a formal brief explaining their decision.[16]   Overall, then, the arbitration procedure was faster and less complicated than a court case, and yet was of the same legal weight.

Over time, as I mentioned, these special courts, called on occasion "*beit din hedyotot*, " were encouraged as a way for Jewish litigants to avoid going to non-Jewish, government courts and thereby keep the resolution of community disputes within the Jewish community. This seems to have been especially the case in which a small community had no recognized legal authorities who could constitute a formal *beit din*.   As an example of how this worked, note the citation from the Codes:

"Whoever appoints a judge, one who is not qualified or is not knowledgable in the knowledge of Torah and is not suitable to be a judge, even if he is very observant and he has other positive attributes, lo the one who appoints him violates a negative command. GLOSS: and it is forbidden to appoint an *am ha-aretz* even on condition that he will confer regularly with a sage. But as for villages that do not have sages suitable to be judges or in which everyone is an *am ha-aretz* but which need judges to adjudicate between them so that they will not go to courts of the gentiles should appoint the best and wisest among them even if they are not suitable to be judges. Since the villagers agreed among themselves to accept these appointees, no one is able to countermand their rulings. Thus any community can accept for itself a court that is not suitable according to Torah."[17]

The practice in Europe, then, as reflected in Isserles' gloss is that non-rabbinic courts could be empaneled, and their decisions had legal weight if no alternative was readily available. In such a case, it was possible to appoint a court of non-judges, but arbiters, whose decision would still be binding. In this case the *halakhah*, as it were, was legitimately articulated by non-rabbinic community members not acting as a *beit din*.[18] This introduces a flexibility in making and shaping local *halakhah* that has rarely been recognized in the recent polemics over what constitutes an *halakhic* Judaism.

Such courts gradually became an accepted feature of the Jewish legal landscape.[19] The institution was in fact adopted early in the twentieth century by the Zionist movement in an attempt to establish some kind of Jewish legal autonomy in the *Yishuv*. The institutional basis was established by the Palestine office of the Zionist Organization in 1909, under the name "*Mishpat HaShalom HaIvri*." Interestingly its first secretary was S. Y. Agnon.[20] This body continued to function into the 1930's.

What this brief survey shows us is that there is a long tradition in rabbinic Judaism of accepting arbitration outside the formal rabbinic *beit din* and of according those decisions, even if promulgated by lay leaders, *halakhic* status. The *halakhah* was not seen to be only the professional legal creation of the rabbinic elite, but just as much the creation of the community in its day-to-day dealings. It offers a perfectly acceptable source of Jewish practice and norms that could exist outside the formal rabbinate. The openness and flexibility represented by this arrangement has unfortunately been totally ignored in the contemporary debate as to the character of the *halakhic* process. Such panels may offer a productive model for how progressive Judaism might undertake the task of creating its own *halakhah*.

THE RABBI AS ARBITER

Notes

1. On this see Boaz Cohen, *Jewish and Roman Law*, Vol. 2, New York, pp. 651ff.

2. M. Sanhedrin 3.1f.

3. According to Asher Gulak, *Yesodei HaMishpat HaIvri*, Vol IV, Jerusalem, 1923, p. 30, the creation of this type of court, technically called a *beth din shel bor'rim*, was devised by R. Meir in response to the repression of Hadrian who enacted a series of measures to restrict Jewish autonomy.

4. M. Sanhedrin 3.1.

5. *Ibid.*, 3.1.

6. J. Sanhedrin 3.1 (21a). The translation is by Jacob Neusner in *The Talmud of Jerusalem: A Preliminary Translation and Explanation, Vol 31*, Chicago, 1984, pp. 96-97.

7. Hoshen Mishpat 12.2; See also Elliot Dorff and Arthur Rosett, *A Living Tree: The Roots and Growth of Jewish Law*, Albany, 1988, p. 294.

8. Asher Gulak, *op. cit.*, p. 26.

9. "At different times and in different countries of the Diaspora, arbitration continued to serve as a substitute for judicial autonomy, in particular where such autonomy had been weakened." Menahem Elon, "Arbitration" in *EJ*, Jerusalem, 1972, Vol. 3, p. 295.

10. Zechariah 8.16.

11. B. Sanhedrin 6b; translation based on Neusner, *op. cit.*, p. 292.

12. B. Sanhedrin 5b; translation based on Neusner, *op. cit*, p. 293.

13. *Otzar HaShatarot HaNehugim BeYisrael*, Jerusalem, 1926. A selection of these are presented in translation in Dorff, *op. cit.*, pp. 295-298.

14. For example, *Panim Me'irot* II: 159. Cited by Elon, *op. cit.*, p. 297.

15. One example of this is found in Majer Balaban, "Die Krakower Judengemeinde - Ordnung von 1595 und ihre Nachtraege" in *JJLG*, Vol. X, 1912, pp. 333-334. The passage is in Yiddish and stipulates that "when the litigants appoint arbiters (*nehmn bor'rim*), the arbiters must sit within twenty-four hours (*miet laet*) and they must make and end of matters within 3 days...."

16. Elon. *op. cit.*, p. 299, cites one salient exception allowed by M. M. Krochmal in the seventeenth century.

17. *Shulhan Arukh*, Hoshen Mishpat 8.1.

18. Salo Baron argues that there was even encouragement for lay participation. See his *A Social and Religious History of the Jews*, New York, 1952, Vol II, p. 267.

19. A fuller discussion is in Menahem Elon's Introduction to *The Principles of Jewish Law*, Jerusalem, 1975, pp. 21f. The rules of the Krakow community mentioned in the preceding note did place some restrictions on who could be appointed to such a court. In particular it banned community leaders. Baron, *op. cit.*, p. 334.

20. See Elon, *op. cit.*, p. 38.

RABBINIC AUTHORITY - POWER SHARING

Old and New Formulas

Walter Jacob

The American synagogue is an eminently democratic institution. Its boards and committees vote on a wide variety of issues. Such complete democracy is, of, course, at variance with the official traditional view of rabbinic authority. According to it, every aspect of human life is governed by obedience to God and the necessary guidance is provided by the Written Law and Oral Law entrusted into the hands of rabbinic interpreters; the scholars might in fact vote but within the parameters of tradition which carried the day. It is somewhat akin to a statement made about Abraham Lincoln who queried his cabinet on an issue and they took a united stand against him. He took the opposite view and indicated that although it was a vote of ten to one, the action would follow the single vote.

The rabbinic ideal has been taught in the literature for the last two thousand years and it is ever present as a basic substrata of all action taken by the rabbinate. As the uncontested arbiters of the Divine tradition, their voice should rule Jewish life and the Jewish people.

Although this may have represented the rabbinic dream, it has never been the reality. The American synagogue with its power sharing between the rabbi and the congregation has been reflected to a greater of lesser degree throughout our long history. Compromises and concessions have been made on both sides in all ages. They reflect the strength of the lay community or the rabbinate. The struggle and tension was often destructive, but as seen over the long span of the centuries it represents one of the most creative forces within Judaism. This tension between the various forms of leadership which have been built into the system has brought renewal and new ideas. It has also led to the survival of the rabbinate as a unique institution able to modify itself and to share its power.

The rabbinate was an ingenious invention of post-Biblical Judaism. It has no Biblical roots or antecedents. As an institution it changed through the ages; it provided at a minimum the basic guidance needed to survive, but in many periods much more.

The Biblical Period

There was, of course, a Biblical precedent for the struggle between the secular and religious forces as one may see in the continuous animosity between the kings of Israel and the outspoken prophets. The lines, however, were not clearly drawn for the official religious representatives, the priests, who were part of the royal entourage. When they played a role in the inner palace intrigue it is not clear whether they were fighting for religious power or only as part of a palace clique. Sometimes they were kingmakers and on other occasions simply a minor force. When the High Priest, along with the prophet, sought to establish Solomon on the throne as David approached death, how much was it an effort for a stronger religious voice? Was the rapid construction of the Temple by Solomon a result of this support? Was the later view of Solomon as a religious author a part of this picture? Although the lines of battle between the kings of Israel and the great prophets, who spoke for social justice and against idolatry and foreign alinements, were clear and sharp, this was not a fight over power within the community as none of these prophetic figures wished to exercise the prerogatives of the king. They simply sought to redirect the royal policy along religious lines.

Talmudic Period

The struggle becomes clearer when we enter the Talmudic

age. As Jacob Neusner has pointed out,[1] it had its roots in the earlier Persian and Arsacid Empire. But we hear only vague echoes and nothing definite about that. In the Sassanian period the Jewish community along with other minority communities within the empire exercised a good deal of self government. They were left autonomous as long as these minority populations were loyal and quiet. The Jewish secular power lay in the hands of the Exilarch. This ruler claimed his authority through Davidic descent. The position was sometimes directly hereditary while at the other times different branches of the family produced a new leader. During the centuries, there were long periods in which the Exilarch and the rabbinic leaders of the great academies got along very well. At other periods there was intense strife over political power. One of the problems for the rabbinate during these periods of struggle was the claim of Davidic descent of the Exilarch; which lent power and prestige, particularly in the eyes of the general population ("The scepter shall not depart from Judea nor a law giver from between his feet").[2] Such descent could hardly be challenged by rabbinic authority.

The accounts of struggles have come down to us in the form of anecdotes and historic reminiscences often vague and altered through long periods of transmission. For much of the chronology we are dependent on the account of Sherira Gaon.[3] Many of these battles centered around the appointment of the heads of the great rabbinic schools. Eventually the Exilarch succeeded in obtaining the right to make those appointments. He thus gained control over the rabbinate and through it a large number of the judicial appointments throughout the empire and in the subsequent period in more distant lands as well. The bad treatment of rabbis by Exilarchs is mentioned in various places in the Talmud.[4] All of this led to strong expressions of dislike on the part of some rabbinic authorities for the Exilarch.[5] As Neusner points out, at the end of the Talmudic Period when the Exilarch had control over the surviving academies, the members of his family attended those academies. This brought the Exilarch and the rabbinate closer together. The alliance was uneasy, and considerable tension always remained. Presumably this state of affairs continued during the subsequent period of the early Islamic Empires under the Caliphate which began in 651.

We know that at least once in the early period of the Caliphate an Exilarch was challenged. This occurred with Bustanai. It was suggested that he was not of true Davidic descent as his mother may have been a Persian princess. The accusations were made and vigorously denied. The documentation which we possess is not clear, but despite the great debate the Exilarch remained in power.[6]

Saboraic and Gaonic Period

In the post Talmudic period of the Saboraim the struggle continued, although we see it only in a shadowy manner through the account of Sherira Gaon. We know that in 658 C.E. the great Academy of Sura was given autonomy and the same occurred to the Academy of Pumbedita in 830 C.E. Earlier both schools had been subjected to the control of the Exilarch.[7] During the period in which the Exilarch ruled over the academies, there were occasional rivalries for the position of Exilarch in which the rabbinate participated. Sometimes each contestant appointed a head of an academy that effectively divided the rabbinate. We hear a good deal of those efforts particularly at Pumbedita as this was Saadiah's own academy and its history interested him more than that of Sura.[8]

We see the struggle between the Exilarch and the gaonate break out vigorously with the appointment of Saadiah by the Exilarch as head of the Academy of Sura. The Exilarch soon discovered that this powerful learned figure would cause him a great deal of trouble. A major division among the political forces ensued. The bitter enmity lasted for several years and involved mutual excommunications as well as the removal of minor officials from judiciaries. It eventually led to Saadiah's removal but only after the entire matter had been brought to the attention of the Caliph. Upon the ascent of a new Caliph in 932 the Exilarch emerged victorious over Saadiah. This was not the end of the matter. A reconciliation between the Exilarch and Saadiah occurred but that was followed by another difficult period which lasted until Saadiah's death in 942.

This episode, which has been preserved in more vivid detail, demonstrates that the struggle for power is more vigorous when an unusual figure emerges and the general authority is less centralized than it had been in the tight knit community of Babylonia.

Early Ashkenazic Communities

As we look at the relationship between the secular Jewish authorities and the rabbinate after the decline of the Gaonate in the rising communities of northern Europe, we see that it depends very much on the size of the community and whether it was new or old. For example, in northern France of the eleventh and twelfth centuries we find no conflicts between the rabbinic authorities and secular Jewish authorities as these communities were very small and there was room for only one source of authority. This was partially due to the fact that the professional rabbinate had not yet fully developed. The communities seemed to be governed by knowledgeable leaders who permitted some democracy. The rabbis who governed the religious life also took care of the communal issues, judicial questions and represented the Jewish community to the Christian rulers.[9] They used the *herem* (excommunication) to enforce their decrees on the community,[10] and other punishments from time to time as well. In all of this they do not appear to have been challenged by any secular Jewish authorities. Similarly, charities were organized entirely through the synagogue community.[11]

The vigorous leadership given by Meir of Rothenburg shows that rabbinic leadership was unchallenged in this period, in that area.[12] Sometimes the government appointed a Jewish merchant to look after its relations with the Jewish community. This position, however, never became particularly powerful and the community did its best to see to it that no one lobbied to obtain such an appointment. This period in northern France saw the rabbinate as supreme and unchallenged. When the Black Death eliminated many Jewish communities in Germany, the smaller communities relied more and more on the few remaining rabbinic scholars. Thus, in the fifteenth century we see rabbinic authority dominant.

From the thirteenth century onward, rabbis in Germany exercised greater authority. This was confirmed by Joel Sirkes[13] who felt that the rabbi should also be compensated appropriately.

Early Sephardic Communities

Matters were quite different in the contemporary Spanish Jewish communities. There, as shown by the responsa of Simon Zemah Duran and Solomon ben Adret, an oligarchical aristocracy took local communal power into its own hands.[14]

A rather thorough picture of communal life emerges from the thousands of responsa of Solomon ben Adret. We see a community in the latter part of the thirteenth century and in the early fourteenth century which was tightly organized and largely under the guidance of a group of *berurim* (lit. clear minded). These individuals, although elected by the community, were essentially an aristocracy and were charged with all communal responsibilities; they appointed other communal officials as well as the judiciary and dealt with the communal property and charity. The election procedure was recorded as closely supervised and democratic. The upper echelons of the community voted. The status of the rabbi and his relationship with the *berurim* is not clear. We do, however, know that the *herem* was invoked by both groups. *Taqanot* protected the honor of the rabbi. Excommunication could result from infringements of their rights.

If we move to the nearby society of North Africa in the fourteenth century we find a distinctive difference between the old native communities and the new Spanish immigrant settlements. The former were governed by a *zaqen* (elder) appointed by the secular government. He had complete power over the rabbinate. The immigrants' community was ruled more democratically, as we learn from Simon ben Zemah Duran. Yet, even in that community *taqanot* could be passed independently without approval of the rabbinate and the *herem* could be applied without their consent.[15]

David Ibn Abi Zimra provided a description of the new immigrant communities of Turkey in the late fourteenth and early fifteenth centuries. All were recent exiles from Spain and so organized themselves according to local Iberian traditions. The *qehillah* (community) was a separate entity responsible for its own internal affairs as well as some charitable ventures. It was governed by a group of *parnasim* [leaders (of a community)] who were either elected by the community or who appointed their own successors.

Each *qehillah* in Turkey selected its own rabbi and pledged itself to support that individual in every way including attending his services, utilizing his judicial decisions and listening to his sermons.[16] However, the rabbi had to gain the consent of the community before he was given communal control. It is unclear to what extent the various rules and regulations (*taqanot*) were passed by the community leaders (*parnasim* or *berurim*) or with the rabbinate. Occasionally the *parnasim* had to decide a conflict between rabbis who claimed authority over a community.

WALTER JACOB

Late Middle Ages

If we return to northern Europe in the fifteenth century, we shall see that in some instances rabbis predominated, in other situations *parnasim* prevailed.[17] But in the late fifteenth and early sixteenth centuries this changed because a professional rabbinate had developed there. The reason for the change was the separation of powers that developed between the *parnasim* and the rabbis. The *parnasim* dealt with taxation and relations with the secular government while the rabbis dealt with purely religious matters as well as internal conflicts between members of the Jewish community. As the *parnasim* usually came from the wealthiest members of the community, they ruled without much concern for the rabbis or anyone else who got in their way. However, in the seventeenth century we find Jewish knowledge among the laity of Central Europe diminishing; this increased the power of the rabbis who were also recognized by the Christian rulers. The rabbis, however, did not wish to have too much contact with the secular powers and in some matters shared authority with lay courts.[18] Occasionally there was some democracy. Nevertheless perpetuation of power from one generation to the next was frequent.

Some of the detailed statutes reveal the division of power among various groups. The appointment of communal officials and the distribution of charity were the most disturbing areas of conflict.[19] There were other problems; for example, when the king or a secular ruler appointed the rabbi with the authority to preside over the uppermost level of the court system.

In sixteenth century Poland, the autonomy of the Jewish community was confirmed by the monarch as demonstrated by the great charter of 1551.[20] This document indicates some power sharing as it mentions "rabbi, judge or other Jewish elders." In this community, rabbi and laity shared power and each had a basis for a claim to authority. The rabbi claimed authority from the

90

traditions of the past while the laity from the power which wealth and status provided. Various efforts were made to strengthen the power of the rabbinate or to at least avoid conflict. However, Joel Sirkes saw to it that some limited power continued in the hands of the laity. He wished, however, to retain ultimate control over each community for the rabbi.[21] Joel Sirkes, Moses Isserles and Solomon Luria restrained the power of the laity by stating that the lay judges should not exceed their limited knowledge.[22]

In Germany in the fifteenth century and later, efforts were made to deal with broad communal questions through synods. Almost all of these contained representatives of both the rabbinate and the laity. The texts themselves, therefore, indicated the kind of compromises worked out. A greater problem was that of the "Court Jew" who had the ear of the ruler but operated outside the normative framework of the Jewish community.[23] Here the rabbinate and the laity, which was less powerful, tried to unite in order to defend themselves against such individuals. Some "Court Jews" were unwilling to recognize the jurisdiction of a rabbinic court and so it was extremely difficult to deal with these powerful, wealthy Jews. This problem arose again and again as various synods attempted to deal with it and with the attendant issues of taxation and rights of settlement.[24] In the sixteenth century, lay leaders such as Josel of Rosheim emerged and the struggle with the "Court Jew" became serious. We should remember that some were learned, a few were rabbis, but most were able business leaders.

From the Emancipation to the Present Time

The clash between rabbinic authority and lay power becomes most easily documented in Napoleon's *Assembly of Notables and Sanhedrin*.[25] There we find a large group of laymen and a small number of rabbis who struggled to answer the questions posed by Napoleon. In issues which were clearly religious, the rabbinate prevailed or managed to work out an appropriate compromise; for example, the recognition of civil marriage and divorce. In other areas the rabbinate was not successful in defending tradition. Such issues were frequently raised later throughout Europe in settings less elaborate and not as well documented as this large meeting. We find echoes of such struggles in every country of Europe. In the nineteenth century this became aggravated through other divisions which made it more difficult to draw sharp lines of distinction between the rabbi and the laity. The debate between Reform and Orthodox, among various secular groups and religious movements and between Zionists and anti-Zionists all too often clouded the issues of power as the struggles involved the rabbinate and laity on both sides.

We find some of these issues emerging more clearly, especially when the Prussian government debated the official position of the rabbi within the Jewish community regarding his right to vote or to veto on boards.[26] Such legislation was enacted in Prussian legislation and later in other German states. We also see the tendency to secede in order to retain rabbinic council as with Samson Raphael Hirsch. We find similar kinds of debate emerge with the development of the chief rabbinate in England. It was not only a debate between the rabbi and his *dayyanim* (judges) and, therefore, an argument over the direction which Orthodoxy should take, but also between the rabbinate and the powerful, wealthy lay figures as may be seen by looking through the issues of the *London Jewish Chronicle* over the decades.

The United States

In the United States we find matters very much affected by the new status of the community. When it began there was no rabbinic leadership whatsoever and so all power rested in the hands of the laity.[27] As rabbis, both traditional and Reform, arrived in the United States, they found that no organizations aside from small local congregations existed. These were led by individuals who had only the scantiest Jewish background and who were not accustomed to the restraint of tradition. If we restrict our view to the Reform community, we shall see that in an effort to gain a broader hold on the community Isaac Mayer Wise founded *The American Israelite* which quickly became an influential paper. As an astute organizer he strengthened the rabbinate through the Hebrew Union College and the Central Conference of American Rabbis. He also recognized the need for lay leadership by earlier establishing the Union of American Hebrew Congregations. The same kind of pattern can be traced in the Conservative and Orthodox Jewish communities.

As the lay leadership acquired power in the general community, they sought it in the Jewish community as well. This was accomplished through new organizations like the Board of Deputies, the American Jewish Committee, as well as the Zionist organizations. Lay leaders like Jacob Schiff, Felix Warburg and Louis Brandeis emerged. They, however, continued to find strong resilient rabbinic leadership. For example, Abba Hillel Silver, Stephen S. Wise, Judah Leon Magnes and Barnett Brickner -all Zionists- emerged as powerful national figures. Here we, however, see the rabbinate entirely outside of its traditional role which was judiciary, ritual or legal. It now played a major political role in matters of both national and internal Jewish policy.

In the latter part of the twentieth century we see the Jewish Federations and similar organizations emerge as planners for the broader Jewish community. Power sharing is the model. Although elected lay leaders are usually at the helm of the organization, the structure is often in the hands of the rabbis who have achieved that position both through their knowledge of tradition and their leadership position. This means that the ongoing guidance is often in the hands of the rabbinate and provides considerable powers to these individuals as well as to other rabbis allied to them.

Many factors play a role in the struggle between laity and rabbinate. Each Jewish civilization has worked out its own scheme for dealing with the ongoing struggle over power and rights. The positions have never been stationary, always fluid and always changing. It is to the credit of the rabbinate that it has been able to change with the times and adjust to the different settings and thus able to maintain the influence of tradition.

As one looks over the struggle through the centuries, one can come to two conclusions:

1. It is clear that the rabbinate has been resilient and able to incorporate within its framework whole areas which were not originally intended.

2. It grew, after the Babylonian Diaspora, into a leadership which often represented the Jewish community within the broader general community, and in the last two centuries has been expanded far beyond those horizons both within and outside the Jewish community. Thus, as an institution, it has proven to be remarkably adaptive.

The continuing struggle between rabbis and laity have kept the Jewish communities somewhat democratic. The tendency for haughty dominance existed on both sides but neither side was ever able to take this too far without considerable opposition from the rest of the community and from the countervailing force. The very rivalry which sometimes caused difficulties was also a source of enormous strength for the community. As rabbis were constantly recruited from the general community, this meant that no rabbinic leader could wander too far afield from the interests of that community.

Notes

1. *Israel Politics in Sassanian Iran - Jewish Self Government in Talmudic Times*, New York, 1986 and earlier studies.

2. Genesis 49.10, as quoted in B. Sanhedrin 5a.

3. *Iggeret Rav Sherira Gaon*, (ed.) B.M. Lewin, Haifa, 1921.

4. B. Gittin 67b; B. Avodah Zarah 38b; B. Shabbat 58a, 121b.

5. B. Sanhedrin 38a; B. Shabbat 54b.

6. Henry Malter, *Saadia Gaon His Life and Works*, Philadelphia, 1921, pp. 96ff.

7. *Ibid.*, p.100.

8. Heinrich Graetz, *Geschichte* V, Leipzig, 1905-1906, Note 12 #7; Malter, *op. cit.,* p. 104.

9. Moritz Gudemann, *Geschichte des Erzieungswesen* , Vol. 1, p. 14; Irving A. Agus, *The Heroic Age of Franco-German Jewry*, pp. 256ff.

10. *Tosafot* to B. Shebuot 29b; B. Makkot 11b.

11. *Tosafot* to B. Ketubot 49b; Semag II 53a.

12. Irving A. Agus, *Meir of Rothenburg*, Philadelphia, 1947, p .

13. Joel Sirkes *Responsum* #52.

14. Leopold Zunz, *Zur Geschichte und Literatur,* Berlin 1845, pp. 513ff; Isidore Epstein, *Studies in the Communal Life of the Jews of Spain,* New York, 1968, p. 33.

15. Isidore Epstein, *The Responsa of Rabbi Simon ben Zemah Duran,* London, 1930, pp. 69f.

16. Israel M. Goldman, *The Life and Times of David Ibn Abi Zimra,* New York, 1970, p. 90.

17. Shlomo Eidelberg, *Jewish Life in Austria* , Philadelphia, 1962, pp. 61ff.

18. Joseph Colon, *Responsa* #169; *Shulhan Arukh, Orah Hayim* 696.8.

19. Myer S. Lew, *The Jews of Poland,* London, 1944, pp. 80ff.

20. Elijah Judah Schochet, *Rabbi Joel Sirkes - His Life, Works and Times,* New York, 1971, pp. 139ff.

21. *Responsa* #32; Mayer of Lublin *Responsa* #62; Joel Sirkes *Responsa* #43.

22. Solomon Luria, *Responsa* #93; Moses Isserles, *Responsa* #33; Joel Sirkes, *Responsa* #51.

23. Selma Stern, *The Court Jew,* Philadelphia, 1950, pp. 177ff.

24. Eric Zemer, *Jewish Synods in Germany During the Latest Middle Ages,* New York, 1978, p. 104.

25. Simon Schwarzfuchs, *Napoleon, The Jews and the Sanhedrin, London, 1979*; Tama, *Transaction of the Parisian Sanhedrin*, London, 1807.

26. B. Jacob, *Die Stellung des Rabbiners.*

27. Jacob R. Marcus, *United States Jewry 1776-1985,* Detroit, 1989.

MINHAG AND HALAKHAH

Toward a Model of Shared Authority on Matters of Ritual

Mark Washofsky

A friend of mine is the *gabai* of an orthodox synagogue in my neighborhood. Assisting him are several *ba'alei batim* known collectively as the "ritual committee." They supervise the many details, both great and small, of their congregation's religious life, and there is always much to do. They hand out the *aliyot* and other honors, determining who shall *daven* and *lein* at every service, especially on the *yamim tovim*. They see to it that the *siddurim* are in good shape, the *talesim* clean and their *tzitzit* kosher, the *yahrzeit* lists up-to-date. They make sure that wine and schnapps are provided for Shabbat, that the *lulav* and *etrog* are ordered in time for *Sukkot*, that the kitchen is closed up before *Pesah* and that the white *parokhet* and Torah mantles are in place at *Selihot*. Their authority over matters of ritual, the dominant aspect of their synagogue's activity, is clear; although many complain about this or that decision, nobody can successfully challenge a ruling of the ritual committee. Nobody, that is, except the rabbi who in this *halakic* community has the final say on all such issues. Moreover, there are a host of ritual questions over which the ritual committee has no say at all. It is the rabbi and not the ritual committee who decides whether the congregants shall stand during every recitation of *qaddish* (they do), whether a *Bat Mitzvah* ceremony can be held in the sanctuary (it cannot), and how high the *mehitzah* shall be currently at the eye-level of the men while seated, but it may soon be raised). Again, people can complain, as they frequently do, about the rabbi's particular decisions. But they do not contest his authority to make them. The congregants accept this division of authority between rabbi and laity, and there is general agreement as to which ritual questions lie on either side of the dividing line.

The situation in liberal congregations is, of course, quite different. The liberal rabbi is seldom the *mara d'atra* whose rulings on questions of synagogue observance claim the status of definitive *p'saq*. In our communities responsibility over ritual matters is shared, rather than divided, between rabbinic and lay leadership. That is, questions which in the orthodox synagogue are the exclusive domain of rabbinic judgement are, in the liberal synagogue, passed upon by the congregation, usually represented through its ritual committee, as well as the rabbi. Liberal Judaism emphasizes the concepts of religious pluralism and autonomy, doctrines which are not particularly compatible with rabbinic *halakhic* authority. Then too, especially on the American scene, the democratic political ideology greatly influences ideas of synagogue governance; the majority rule principle often overcomes the traditional Jewish tendency to submit questions of ritual to rabbinic adjudication.[1] Finally, the ritual committee often embodies the congregation's concern for the preservation of its own traditions against the well-meaning interference of a rabbi who, however, beloved by the community, is not *of* the community.

Liberal rabbis acknowledge that their role is not, in the main, that of *poseq*, and some renounce on theological grounds even the slightest claim of "authority" over the congregation. Still, shared authority over ritual matters frequently provokes tensions between them and their laity. The liberal rabbi, no less than his or her orthodox colleague, serves the congregation as its resident expert in Judaica. By virtue of academic training and practical experience, the rabbi can justifiably claim that issues of liturgical and ceremonial observance fall within the area of his or her professional competence. As a professional, the rabbi will likely view ritual matters from a perspective other than that of the laity. And as a professional, the rabbi will become perplexed or distressed when the laity, asserting power within the traditional domain of the rabbi-scholar, make decisions which in the rabbi's eyes contradict some higher principle or value of Jewish religious practice. Given this arrangement--shared authority among those of substantially differing points of view--conflict between liberal rabbis and their congregations over ritual issues can scarcely be avoided.

If the sharing of authority over matters of ritual is more characteristic of liberal than of orthodox communities, it is hardly a new phenomenon in Jewish religious history. Broadly speaking, the roots of Jewish observance are to be found in one of two major sources: *halakhah*, "lawyer's law," the rules and principles, both Toraitic and rabbinic, developed in the Babylonian Talmud and interpreted and applied by an elite class of scholars, the *talmidei hakhamim*; and *minhag*, "people's law," practices which originate in community custom and usage.[2] The validity of *halakhah*, the more formal of the two, depends upon its location in a discrete judicial or legislative act: it is derived from existing texts through the process of *midrash* or legislated by means of rabbinic *taqanah* or *gezerah*. As such, *halakhah* has been the province of the scholars entrusted with the interpretation of the *Torah*, with "building a fence" around the *Torah*, and with the preservation of oral traditions which claim Toraitic force. *Minhag*, by contract, has no such precise beginnings. It is simply the long-standing custom of the people,[3] a practice that originated outside the walls of the *yeshivah* and developed independently of the formal, logical rules of rabbinic law. This difference in origin has not resulted in an irreparable conflict within Jewish law. On the contrary, the rabbis over the centuries have developed means by which to integrate *minhag* in the *halakhic* system. They have, first of all, extended their supervision over the *minhagim*, to determine that they are of valid pedigree (*minhag vatiqin*) and that they do not violate the boundaries of logic, reasonability and *halakhah*.[4] Once they have determined that a custom is not forbidden on these grounds, rabbinic authorities have permitted it to operate freely in "neutral spaces" in the law, where *minhag* either does not or need not conflict with formal *halakhah*. This is especially true of *dinei mamonot*, monetary law, where it is presumed that the rules are set for the mutual convenience of the parties,[5] but it applies as well to some areas of ritual practice, such as liturgical *nusah* and the selection of *haftarot*, where no *halakhic* requirement interferes with the community's choice.[6]   In some instances where the formal *halakhah* is either forgotten or disputed, *minhag* is allowed decisory power.[7]   Again, this power is justified by a theoretical argument: the existence of an established custom is evidence of a *halakhah* which actually originated in some more formal source (*midrash*, *taqanah*, etc.,).   Even when a *minhag* appears to contradict the *halakhah*, rabbinic authorities may not rush to denounce it.   At such times integration becomes accommodation, as *halakhists* seeking to defend the practice of their community reinterpret the formal legal rules so that the practice, hallowed by time and custom, no longer violates *halakhic* principle.   A well-known example concerns *yom edeihem shel goyim*, the festival days of Gentiles. The prevailing custom of Jewish merchants in medieval Europe was to do business with their Gentile neighbors on these days, even though such was a clear violation of *halakhah*.[8] Yet, the rabbis of northern Europe found arguments with which to justify this custom, which at least one of them termed "astonishing."[9]   Their willingness to do so, in this and in other cases, has been attributed to a conviction on their part that *minhag avoteinu Torah*: the ancestral customs of a holy community, customs sanctified by years of usage, cannot truly violate the *Torah*, even though they seem to do just that.[10]   Practice, as well as abstract law, is understood as being informative of God's will. As God's will is a unity, so too can there be no essential contradiction between the obligations enunciated in the texts of *halakhah* and those which have grown up in the dynamic of religious life. If contradictions nonetheless appear, the scholar-rabbis will undertake to harmonize and to accommodate their elite, intellectual *halakhah* with the folk religion of the Jews, observance born in the laboratory of life.

I want to argue that this aspect of Jewish legal history can serve as guidance for today's communities struggling with the ambiguities of shared ritual authority. That is, while rabbis and laity must both pass on the same religious issues, each side has its own distinct role to play in the determination of practice. The rabbi, in the liberal as well as the orthodox setting, is the authority of textbook law, the scholar who declares and interprets for the congregation the rules and principles that govern the institutions of Jewish observance. The laity, for its part, is the creator and guardian of *minhag*, a thoroughly legitimate source of Jewish law. Neither side, in other words, needs to be "boss." The task of both is to maintain the conversation between *halakhah* and *minhag* which has a long and honored history in the literature of rabbinic law. The following three examples can help illustrate this conversation, the encounter between religious observance produced by the dynamic of Jewish life and the existing *halakhah* as understood by the community's teachers.

1. *HALLEL ON ROSH HODESH.*

R. Yohanan said in the name of R. Shimeon b. Yehotzadaq: on eighteen days an individual recites the entire (*gomer bahen*) *Hallel*. They are: the eight days of *Hanukah*, the first day of *Pesah*, and *Shavuot*. In the diaspora, there are twenty-one days (counting an extra day of *yom tov* for *Shemini Atzeret*, the first day of *Pesah*, and *Shavuot*).[11]

This requirement, understood by most authorities as a rabbinic *taqanah*,[12] does not apply to the remaining days of *Pesah* and to *Rosh Hodesh*. The Talmud explains that the concluding days of *Pesah*, unlike the intermediate days of *Sukkot* and *Shemini Atzeret*, are not distinguished one from the other in the number of sacrifices to be offered; *Rosh Hodesh*, meanwhile, is not a "*hag*," a day on which work is forbidden. For this reason, the early amora Rav, was surprised when, coming to Babylonia from *Eretz Yisrael*, he saw the people recite *Hallel* on *Rosh Hodesh*. He intended to protest this practice, but when he saw that only the half-*Hallel*

(*Hallel bedilug*) was recited, he concluded that "such is their ancestral custom (*minhag avoteihem b'yadam*)." The Talmud[13] concludes by citing a *baraita* which states than an individual praying alone need not begin the *Hallel*, but if he does he may complete it.

Since Rav allowed this *minhag* to stand, subsequent rabbinic authorities saw no need to suppress it. Still, it caused them no little conceptual difficulty. Although the recitation of *Hallel* was ordained for festival days, as a reminder of God's redemptive acts for Israel,[14] *Rosh Hodesh* is not a festival and commemorates no redemptive acts. The people's practice, in other words, contradicts the liturgical theory behind the *Hallel*, a fact which compelled *halakhic* scholars to search for means to remove this contradiction, to accommodate the *minhag* to the existing *halakhah* and the *halakhah* to it. One way to do this was to construct a systemic justification for *Hallel* on *Rosh Hodesh*, to buttress the custom with text and theory. Thus, the suggestion that this *Hallel* is hinted in the twelve mentions of the word *haleluyah* in Psalm 150,[15] or the more mundane observation that the *Hallel* served as a reminder to the Babylonians that today was *Rosh Hodesh*.[16] A second task was to define and adjust the terms of the *minhag* according to the existing *halakhic* prescriptions for *Hallel*. For example, some *gaonic* authorities had already established that there is no legal distinction to be made concerning *Hallel* between the *yahid* (individual) and the *tzibur* (the *minyan* of ten), when the individual does not complete the *Hallel*, neither does the community.[17] On the other hand, the *baraita* on Ta'anit 28b suggests to others than an individual praying without a *minyan* should not recite *Hallel* at all on *Rosh Hodesh*.[18] Eventually, rabbinic opinion reached a consensus that the individual should indeed recite it.[19] A more difficult issue concerned the *berakhot* before and after the *Hallel*. On other days, when the obligation to recite *Hallel* was based upon a rabbinic ordinance, there was no question that a benediction was to be pronounced, since it is entirely proper to say *v'tzivanu*, "who has commanded us" over a *mitzvah derabanan*.[20] On *Rosh Hodesh*, however, when the recitation of *Hallel* was based on *minhag* and not rabbinic enactment, it was not at all obvious that a *berakhah* should be said. The Talmud[21] relates that no benediction was recited over the beating of the *aravot* precisely because that practice was a *minhag*. Rashi explains that a *minhag* differs from a *taqanah* in that no benediction is to be recited over it; indeed, how can one say "who has commanded us" over an act which was voluntarily adopted by the people and which was not imposed upon them either by the Torah or the rabbis?[22] Such a blessing is a *berakhah l'vatalah*, a violation of the prohibition of taking God's name in vain.[23] This position is held consistently by the "Rashi School"[24] and by Maimonides, who states flatly that "one does not recite a benediction over a *minhag*."[25] On the other hand, the recitation of a *berakhah* over *Hallel* on *Rosh Hodesh* is attested in *gaonic* times[26] and was accepted in northern Europe, where the Tosafists developed theories to justify the practice. R. Ya'aqov Tam argued that the relevant Talmudic passages prove that a benediction was recited. For example, if no *berakhah* were said, Rav would not have thought at first to stop the Babylonians from saying *Hallel*, nor would the Talmud[27] have raised the issue of interruptions during the *Hallel*. Without a benediction, "*Hallel*" is simply the recitation of psalms, to which there can be no particular objection and which may be interrupted. With a *berakhah* it becomes a ritual act, and *halakhic* concerns--*berakhah l'vatalah*, interruptions--are thereby in order. The fact is, he contended, we do say benedictions over *minhagim*, such as the *qiddush* on the second day of *Yom Tov*. As for the *aravah* we cannot compare that practice, the mere shaking of branches, with the *Hallel*, which resembles reading from Torah, over which we do say a *berakhah*.[28]

These arguments over this issue closely paralleled those surrounding a similar *minhag*: the custom among women in Ashkenazic lands to recite benedictions when performing positive, time-bound commandments to which they were neither Toraitically

105

nor rabbinically obligated. Here, too, was an existing practice which appeared to contradict the rules of *halakhah*. How could women, when taking the *lulav* or donning *tefilin*, say the formal "who has commanded us" when it is obvious that they are "commanded" to perform neither of these acts? There could hardly be a greater example of *berakhah l'vatalah*, and the *halakhic* authorities of most regions either forbade the practice[29] or counseled that "it is better for women not to say a benediction."[30] Again, it was the Tosafists who created *halakhic* arguments to support this *minhag*. Rabbenu Tam suggested that the unnecessary *berakhah* is not in fact a violation of Exodus 20.7, and he further compared the case of women to that of blind men, who according to one opinion are exempt from the commandments but still recite the blessing when they perform *mitzvot*.[31] These arguments, as the Tosafists themselves recognized, were somewhat forced.[32]

Seeking to avoid the pitfalls of this analysis, other scholars justified the permit on the grounds that, while one normally receives a greater reward for performing an obligatory than a voluntary act, women who observe the *mitzvot* get some reward for doing so and are thus entitled to say the *berakhah*.[33] This logic, too, is difficult: whatever the merit of their voluntary act, women are still not obliged to observe these *mitzvot*. How then may they say "who has commanded us?" This difficulty is resolved in the laconic statement of R. Moshe of Coucy, who links the benedictions over *Hallel* and the blessings recited by women: "When one wishes to oblige himself to a previously voluntary act, he may recite a benediction. And this is not a *berakhah l'vatalah*."[34] Implicit in this reasoning, perhaps, is the notion that an individual who waives a Toraitic exemption is thereby *metzuveh*, obligated on a par with all others, and falls under the category of "who has commanded us." This would mean that the individual, by personal choice, may exalt a *minhag*, a practice not required under the formal rules of the *halakhic* system, to a statue synonymous with *mitzvah*.[35] At any rate, both practices - benedictions recited by women and the *berakhah* for *Hallel* on *Rosh Hodesh* - prevailed among Ashkenazic

Jews,[36] and both were surrounded by argumentation defending their legitimacy within the *halakhic* system.[37]

2. EVENING *SHEMA* BEFORE SUNDOWN.

The very first Mishnah in tractate Berakhot discusses the time at which the evening *Shema* must be recited. While opinions differ as to the *terminus ad quem* of the *mitzvah*, the *tana'im* agree that the *Shema* should not be said before "the priests enter to eat the *t'ruham*." A *Baraita* equates this time with "the appearance of the stars."[38] This became the accepted *halakhah*.[39] It was not an unheard-of practice to recite the *Shema* before sundown; a *baraita* in the Yerushalmi[40] notes that such is the custom, but stresses that this early recitation does not fulfill the obligation of saying the evening *Shema*. It serves rather as an introduction to the evening prayer, that we might "rise for the *tefilah* after having studied words of Torah." The *gaonim*, as well, record that some communities recite the *Shema* in the synagogue before sundown, but they did not approve of the practice. Rav Hai Gaon ruled that, in a case where the public worship service would in any event take place before sundown, it was preferable to recite the *tefilah* first and then the *k'ri'at Shema* at its proper time, following the appearance of the stars. In this way, one can pray with the community and fulfill the *mitzvah* of *Shema*. Under no circumstance, however, would the recitation of *Shema* before sundown be sufficient.[41]

In northern Europe, the custom to recite the evening *tefilah* before sundown was widely accepted, undoubtedly due to the great amounts of summer daylight in the northern latitudes which made it difficult to gather the congregation after nightfall.[42] The people assembled at the conclusion of the work day (but well before nightfall) to recite *minhah* and *ma'ariv*. The *Shema* was recited in its proper liturgical context, immediately prior to the evening *tefilah*. *Halakhists*, facing this long-standing *minhag* which so obviously contradicted Talmudic law, once again turned to the task of forging a *halakhic* justification for it. Rashi, for example, notes that the one who says the *Shema* in the synagogue before sundown does not fulfill his *halakhic* obligation. Why then do we recite it so early? "To rise for the *tefilah* after having studied words of Torah," as the *Yerushalmi* puts it. "Therefore, we must recite it again after it becomes dark. And the recitation of the first *parashah*,[43] which is the practice at bedtime, is sufficient for this purpose."[44] In this way, Rashi upholds both *minhag* and *halakhah*. He sees nothing wrong with the custom as such and even justifies it, so long as the individual takes care to fulfill his ritual obligation later in the evening. The problem with his approach, as our Tosafot point out,[45] is that if the bedtime *Shema* were in fact the fulfillment of that obligation, we would read all three *parashi'ot* of the *Shema* at that time. We would also pronounce the statutory *berakhot*, two preceding and two following the *Shema*, yet in fact, those blessings are recited in the synagogue before sundown. Moreover, the bedtime *Shema* was ordained as protection against evil spirits, which means that *talmidei hakhamim*, whose Torah is their protection, need not recite it at all. Rather, says Rabbeinu Tam, we must conclude that the recitation of the *Shema* in the synagogue is the actual fulfillment of the *halakhic* obligation. As to why this recitation takes place before sundown, R. Tam turns to an analysis of *M. Berakhot* 4.1, the obligatory times for *tefilah*. We hold according to R. Yehudah, who declares that *minhah* may be recited until *p'lag haminhah*, about 4:45 p.m. on the twelve-hour "sun clock," rather than "until evening," which is the position of the *s'tam mishnah*. As soon as the time period for *minhah* ends, "nighttime" begins for *ma'ariv* and for *k'ri'at Shema*. How then do we account for the custom of reciting the afternoon prayer *after* the time of *p'lag haminhah*. R. Tam replies that since the *s'tam mishnah* holds that *minhah* may be said till dark, and since the Talmud[46] pointedly does not decide between the two positions, we follow both of them: R. Yehudah for *Shema* (so that we may recite it early) and the *s'tam mishnah* for *tefilah* (so that we may recite it after *p'lag haminhah).* The difficulty of this position does not escape the Tosafists, who argue that one ought to follow either the view of R. Yehudah or of the *s'tam mishnah* but not the leniencies of each. In addition, those *tana'im* are disputing the time of *tefilah,* which was set according to the time at which sacrifices were offered in the Temple. The evening *Shema,* by contrast, is to be said "when you lie down," a time which cannot be fixed before sundown. No proof, in other words, can be brought for *Shema* from *minhah.*[47] Rather, says R. Yitzhaq of Dampierre, we recite the evening *Shema* early because we hold that the *halakhah* is according to R. Eliezer and R. Meir, who teach in *beraitot* that the *Shema* may be recited from the time that people begin to observe Shabbat eve; i.e., *before* sundown.[48] Thus, although the accepted view was that the *halakhah* followed M. Berakhot 1.1, that the time for the evening *Shema* begins at sundown, the existence of the established *minhag* indicated to R. Yitzhaq that this understanding was incorrect. The law must follow those sages whose positions accord with our custom.

There is one problem with this analysis: it contradicts some basic rules of *halakhic* decision. In the afore-mentioned *beraitot* R. Eliezer is in dispute with R. Yehoshua and R. Meir with R. Yehudah. According to accepted Talmudic tradition, the law follows the latter authority in both of these cases, and in both, R. Yehoshua and R. Yehudah argue that sundown begins the time of the evening *Shema.*[49] It is clearly for this reason that R. Yehudah Hanasi declares their position as the anonymous (=authoritative, undisputed) view in the first Mishnah. R. Yitzhaq's theory, then, is beset with serious *halakhic* weakness.

We should note that virtually all authorities outside of Ashkenaz reject this custom; "whoever recites the evening *Shema* before the appearance of the stars is saying a *berakhah l'vatalah.*"[50] This does not mean that they *abolished* the custom; indeed, like Rav Hai Gaon, several of them concede that the community practice is firmly entrenched and cannot be changed. They suggest to the observant worshipper various compromises designed to allow him to pray with the congregation and yet recite the *Shema* at its proper time.[51] These "compromises," however, did not indicate *halakhic* approval of the *minhag*: these authorities clearly recognized that the recitation of the *Shema* before sundown does not fulfill one's *halakhic* obligation.

The later *Ashkenazic* authorities, meanwhile, offered a different kind of compromise. The *halakhah*, they acknowledge, does not follow the *tana'im* who allow the evening *Shema* to be recited early. Nonetheless, patterns of communal life decree that we accept their view. The people cannot wait until sundown, quite late in the evening according to the summer clock, to assemble for public prayer. Public prayer, if not Toraitically required, is itself an important religious value. "Therefore, the people are accustomed to recite the *Shema* and pray before the appearance of the stars, relying on these *tana'im*, although in principle, one should not recite the *Shema* until the appearance of stars."[52] These authorities, therefore, draw a distinction between the abstract *halakhah* and *halakhah* in practice. In principle, the evening *Shema* ought to be read after sundown. In the actual circumstances of communal life, however, the *halakhah* must follow the minority opinion, inasmuch as the desire of the community to pray together as a congregation has preserved the *minhag* of early recitation of the *Shema*. The *minhag* thus transforms the nature of rabbinic discourse over the issue. The discussion of the theoretical *halakhah* is accompanied, especially among the *Ashkenazim*, by a rigorous defense of their ancestral custom ("those who reject the words of R. Tam and delay the *Shema* till after sundown are guilty of excessive piety")[53] and by the creation of *halakhic* arguments, however forced they may be, to defend that *minhag* according to the rules of the *halakhic* system. This justification became increasingly difficult; by the fifteenth century, Ashkenazic authorities were complaining that *ma'ariv* was being recited much earlier in the afternoon than even the Tosafists' theories would permit. Despite that fact, the power and prevalence of *minhag* was such that most authorities found ways to preserve the coexistence of custom and *halakhah*.[54]

3. KOHEN CALLED FIRST TO THE TORAH.

The Mishnah[55] tells us that among the things ordained "for the sake of peace" (*mipnei darkei shalom*) was the rule that the *kohen* is called first to the Torah, followed by a Levite and a *yisra'el*. The Talmud[56] lists various *d'rashot* which base this rule upon Scripture; ultimately, the derivation from Leviticus 21.8 ("you shall sanctify him") is accepted. As the *Baraita* says: "Sanctify him (the priest) in all matters pertaining to holiness. Let him speak first, say the blessing first, etc." If so, then the practice must be Toraitic; why then do we say "for the sake of peace," which implies a rabbinic ordinance?[57] The answer, suggested by Abaye, is that the Torah indeed grants the *kohen* priority in these matters. It is the rabbis, however, who "for the sake of peace" ordain that in the synagogue, unlike the other settings, the *kohen* is not entitled to forego this honor and bestow it upon a non-priest. If he were to do so, "quarrels would ensue." Rav Matana limits the exception to Shabbat and festivals; on weekdays, when fewer people are in the synagogue, the priest may forego his honor. The Talmud objects: Did not Rav Huna (a *yisra'el*) read first from the Torah on Shabbat and festivals? The answer: Rav Huna was different, since even R. Ami and R. Asi, the leading *kohanim* of Eretz Yisra'el, recognized his authority.

The early interpretations of this *sugya* deny the priest the right to bestow his priority upon another, even if that other person is a great scholar. The *gaonic* sources declare that "an ignorant *kohen* precedes a *yisra'el* who is a Torah scholar."[58] Other authorities take a different view. R Ya'aqov ben Asher, citing the opinion of his father, suggests that the example of Rav Huna proves

111

that anyone who is distinguished (*muflag*) in Torah learning may be called to the Torah before the *kohen*.[59] R. Shelomo ben Adret (Rashba) refers his correspondent to Megilah 28a, where R. Yohanan declares that "if a scholar allows an ignorant person to precede him in reciting a benediction, even if that person is the High Priest, that scholar is deserving of death." The law, concludes Adret, requires that a scholar precede a *kohen* unless the *kohen* is himself a scholar.[60] R. Yitzhaq b. Sheshet (Rivash) is more explicit. "When the *yisra'el* is a scholar and the priest an ignoramus, the scholar is called first. There is no concern of *mipnei darkhei shalom* in this case. On the contrary, it is a sin if this procedure is not followed." Nonetheless, the *minhag* of "all Israel" is for even an ignorant priest to be called first to the Torah, "and one should not change this *minhag*, since this would lead to contention."[61] A similar view is expressed by Maimonides in his commentary.[62] The priest, he says, does not rank above a Torah scholar. It is scholarship and not *yihus* which rules in these matters. Do we not read that "a *mamzer* who is a scholar takes precedence over a High Priest who is an ignoramus?"[63] Unlike R. Asher, Rambam does not require that this other scholar be a *muflag*; the honor of reading first from the Torah should be bestowed in order of the Torah knowledge of those present in the synagogue. It is only when the *kohen* is equal in knowledge to the *yisra'el* that he is forbidden to forego his honor, "for the sake of peace." Rambam is aware, of course, that custom does not follow what he considers to be the plain meaning of the Talmud text. As opposed to Rivash, however, he goes out of his way to condemn the *minhag*. Noting that in all lands even an ignorant priest precedes a scholar to the Torah, he protests that the practice has no root whatever in the Torah, is not mentioned in the Talmud, and is not the intention of the Mishnah. "I am absolutely astonished," he writes, "that this custom exists as well in the southern regions, whose practice ordinarily conforms to the language of the Talmud and who are not afflicted with the sickness of *minhagim* and of the opinions of recent authorities." Nonetheless, the *minhag* exists, and in his Code, Maimonides seems resigned to the fact that the *minhag* determines practice: "It is the widespread custom today that even an ignorant priest precedes a *yisra'el* who is a Torah scholar."[64]

Although R. Yosef Karo was a great admirer of Rambam, this was too much. In a lengthy analysis of the issue in the *Beit Yosef*,[65] he comments that "we must at least give an explanation to this *minhag*. It has been accepted by every community, and it is not fitting to say that this acceptance has been in error." Karo posits that the *halakhic* arguments offered by Rambam, Rashba, Rivash, and the Tur assume that to allow an ignorant priest to precede a scholar to the Torah is an affront to that scholar's dignity, and *kevod haTorah* must surely override *kevod hakohen*. This is not necessarily the case: "If the rabbis ordained that a priest should be called first to the Torah 'for the sake of peace,' then this is no insult to a scholar." Indeed, "in these times, the great sages do not insist on the honor of being called first." Rather, it is more honorific for them to receive the final *aliyah* to the Torah, "and in this manner, the *kohanim* do not have to forego their honor for the sake of the great scholars." As for the Talmudic sources cited by the earlier authorities, none of these oblige us to overturn the *minhag*. Even if "a *mamzer*, who is a scholar, takes precedence over a High Priest who is an ignoramus," this applies "to everything other than the reading of the Torah," which has been rendered an exception by the *taqanah* "for the sake of peace."

It is tempting to view the debate between Karo and the other scholars as an argument over the correct *halakhic* interpretation of passages such as Gittin 59b, M. Horayot 3.7 and others. We should resist this temptation. Citing a responsum of the fifteenth-century Italian, R. Yosef Kolon, Karo is aware of the latter's view that "all the *posqim* agree that the leading scholar is called first to Torah," and he even struggles to fit the *gaonic* rulings into this category.[66] The *halakhah*, as understood by a long chain of authorities, either allows the priest to give way to the scholar or

113

demands that he do so. The *minhag* followed in all communities[67] denies this option to the priest and to the congregation. Faced with a clear conflict between theoretical law and actual practice, Karo presumes that the *minhag* cannot be false. His purpose is not to refute the opinion of the preponderance of rabbinic scholars but rather to incorporate the widespread *minhag* into the system of Jewish legal thought. The justification he offers the *minhag* does not mean that it accords with the plain sense of the Talmud; it most probably does not. It serves instead to legitimize the practice in *halakhic* terms, so that, regardless of the "best" reading of the Talmudic sources, the custom observed by "all Israel" represents at any rate a *good* one, a *plausible* one that does not necessarily stand in violation of *halakhah*.

This "incorporation" might better be dubbed the "naturalization" of *minhag*. As our analysis of these three examples shows, *minhag* is something of a foreign element within the classic *halakhic* system. *Halakhah* is anchored in the lines of sacred text. The "right" or "correct" *halakhah* is determined by interpretation of the text, a study aimed at rendering the best and most convincing account of the text's words and passages. This search for the "best" and "most convincing" is a process of deductive analysis, the logical explication of the Talmudic *sugya*, the declaration of the law in a code, or the elaboration of a scholar in his commentary or responsum. As is the case with most other legal literatures, the authoritative interpretation of *halakhah* is entrusted to a specially trained body of scholars who possess the requisite intellectual talents to follow the logic of the texts and the religious probity to be recognized as *posqim*, decisors of the law.

The "anchor" of *minhag*, by contrast, is the fact of its continuation within a community over a period of time. Its justification lies not in logic, nor even in a Talmudic text, but in the fact that a particular body of Jews has adopted and held fast to it. Its authority derives not simply from sacred text but from sacred life, from the veneration of ancestral practice, or from a heritage (especially in *Ashkenaz*) of customary ritual observances which exist alongside of and do not owe their origin to the formal *halakhah* of texts and Talmud. *Minhagim* are authoritative not because scholars derive them but because the people observe them, and the people will most likely resent attempts by scholar-rabbis, through their sharp and ingenious textual gymnastics, to prove that the custom of "all Israel" is somehow in error.[68]

It is hardly surprising, then, that the religious life of the Jews in all its complexity has produced numerous *minhagim* which conflict with and are alien to the rational structure of *halakhic* theory. Our three examples are cases in point. From the standpoint of logic, *Hallel* should not be recited on *Rosh Hodesh*, a day on which no salvation was wrought for Israel. The recitation of a *berakhah* over a customary or voluntary observance violates both the theory and the language of this liturgical form. By all textual indications and the rules of *halakhic* decision the evening *Shema* ought not to be recited before sundown. And the relevant Talmudic passages seem to bear out the interpretations of the great *rishonim*: A *kohen* either may or must allow a Torah scholar to precede him to the Torah. *Minhag*, however, is not the product of the rational analysis of formal rules and principles. It springs from what Jacob Katz calls the "ritual instinct" of the people rather than from logical analysis of text.[69] These *minhagim* have attained power and permanence because they genuinely reflect this instinct: the desire to raise the status of a voluntary act to that of *mitzvah*; the desire to pray together as a community even though that gathering can take place only before nightfall; and the desire to render honor to the *kohanim*. The service of these religious impulses led to the creation of ritual practices which violate the formal *halakhah*.

When *halakhic* authorities confront such a *minhag*, they may assume a variety of postures. They may declare it to be a *minhag*

115

ta'ut, a mistaken practice which deserves to be annulled.[70] They may, as we have seen, note that the *minhag* conflicts with the *halakhah* but acknowledge its obligatory force. They may also find Talmudic-*halakhic* justifications for the *minhag*. These justifications, as we have seen, are not entirely persuasive. There is always another point of view, that of the *posqim* who do not accept the validity of the *minhag*, and we somehow cannot escape the feeling that those authorities have the better argument. Often, the "anti-*minhag*" position seems manifestly in closer accord with the sense of the relevant Talmudic passages or with the conceptual framework of the ritual observance in question. In the end, however, the weakness of the "pro-*minhag*" arguments is not decisive. When a *minhag* has existed over time and when it clearly derives from the legitimate "religious instinct" of the people, it is unnecessary to prove that it represents the one "correct" or "best" interpretation of the Talmudic *sugya*. It is sufficient rather to demonstrate that the custom is not forbidden, that it *can* be justified, that a rather plausible theory can be offered in its behalf so that its existence need not contradict the basic parameters of the *halakhah*. Such theories are not difficult to construct. The *halakhic* sources are rich in intellectual intensity and sophistication, and as the vast literature of the Tosafot and *rishonim* amply demonstrates, they afford a virtually limitless range of possibilities for *hiddush* and creative interpretation. Unlike *minhagim*, which are sanctified by tradition and usage prove difficult to change and impossible to annul, the abstract conceptual rules and principles of *halakhah* can be combined, rearranged, and manipulated by a scholar with an agile mind in such a way as to produce a variety of solutions to the same problem. The "most obvious" and the "most plausible" understanding of a text, in other words, does not exhaust its full range of interpretive possibilities. And the *posqim* have frequently abandoned standard, traditionally-accepted interpretations in favor of alternative readings which, though somewhat forced and not as literal, are more congenial to the existence of popular custom. In this way, *minhag* has acted as a spur to *halakhic* dynamism and creativity.

In the tension between *minhag* and *halakhah* lies one of the fundamental distinctions between orthodox and liberal *halakhic* writing. In today's orthodox world, this tension has spent its creative force. *Minhag* has long ceased to be a separate source of law in potential competition with *halakhah*. Both are administered and interpreted by the same elite rabbinic authority, which disallows the innovation of new custom and resists any attempt to critique established *minhagim,* even on the basis of solid *halakhic* argumentation. The experience of the early Reformers who argued on Talmudic grounds against *piyutim* and *Kol Nidrei* and in favor of prayer in the vernacular is instructive in this regard. In our liberal tradition, we have taken a more positive view of the continuing creative power of *minhag.* Liberal *halakhic* scholarship, accordingly, has concentrated heavily upon the "naturalization" of the many practices which exist in our communities and which deviate from the accepted norms of *halakhah.* An outstanding example of this work is R. Solomon B. Freehof's *Reform Jewish Practice,* whose introduction expresses a theory of *minhag* as a living source of Jewish observance. While "the chief purpose (of the book) is to describe present-day Reform Jewish practice and the traditional rabbinic laws from which they are derived," its major focus is upon the justification--*bedi'avad*--of existing practices even when they are *not* derived from rabbinic law.[71] Reminiscent of the *rishonim* Freehof seeks to address the apparently "alien" nature of Reform practice and to "naturalize" it, bringing it under the canopy of the theory of rabbinic law. Many Reform responsa, as well, are marked by this same intellectual process. Ironically, it is the literature of the most "*non-halakhic,*" of today's Jewish groupings which continues the drama, debate, and creative conversation between *halakhah* and *minhag* that fill the most interesting passages of the *halakhic* commentaries, codes, and responsa.

This conversation is alive and well in our congregations.

Put differently, the dichotomy between elite and folk religion which we find in the Talmud and the *halakhic* literature reflects the reality of shared ritual authority between rabbi and ritual committee. And the heritage of this scholarly activity can and should inform the efforts of both. That is, it is the function of the ritual committee to preserve the local *minhag* and to suggest, even in the face of a skeptical rabbinic leader, that the community's observances do represent a tradition of "ritual instinct." The role of the liberal rabbi, while not that of *mara d'atra*, is the same as that of the scholar-rabbi, in the traditional literature: To examine these *minhagim* under the light of *halakhah*, the rules and principles which define and give structure to Jewish observance. This examination need not be a sometime thing. While the committee is the conservative element in this model, the rabbi can take the initiative in bringing the entire range of congregational ritual practice before the committee's attention. The results of this process will be as varied as those in the medieval *halakhic* texts. Under the rabbi's careful guidance and instruction, the congregation may discover that a certain practice stands in sharp contradiction with a higher ritual value. The committee may well determine that the practice is a *minhag ta'ut*, a mistake which carries adverse religious implications. In other instances, the rabbi can explore with the committee the possibility that local custom, though not in his or her opinion the best or most desirable ritual option, can be justified according to the theory, rules, and principles of Jewish observance. The *minhag*, of course, will in all probability survive the failure to arrive at such a justification. Still, the rabbi will have fulfilled the supreme rabbinic duty: to encourage the community to study Torah, to measure the reality of its religious life against the ideal standards taught in text and tradition.

Shared authority in matters of ritual need not be grounds for irresolvable conflict. Indeed, such sharing of authority is well attested in the history of Jewish law, in the creative tension between *halakhah* and *minhag*. As that tension resolved itself in the "naturalization" of *minhag* and the expansion of *halakhah*, so too can conversation between rabbi and ritual committee be a source of religious growth and development in a congregation. All that is required is a laity willing to examine its customs openly and honestly, a rabbi able to interpret Torah in all its fullness and intricacy, and a readiness on all sides to teach and learn from each other.

Notes

1. This factor is not limited to liberal congregations. Numerous "orthodox" synagogues of a previous generation resolved knotty ritual controversies--such as the battle over mixed seating--by submitting them to a vote of the membership rather than to the binding *halakhic* decision of the rabbi.

2. On the "legal sources of Jewish law," see the comprehensive treatment by Menachem Elon, *Hamishpat Ha-Ivri*, Jerusalem, 1978. His discussion of *minhag* is found on pp. 713-767.

3. To be legally obligatory, a *minhag* must be "a common practice, performed frequently," (Isserles, *Shulhan Arukh*, Hoshen Mishpat 331.1), and officially declared by the community's scholars to be the accepted practice (*Arukh Hashulhan*, Hoshen Mishpat 331 #5).

4. See the rules and qualifications discussed in R. Haim Hizkiah Medini, *S'dei Hemed*, V. 4, pp. 74-109.

5. On the relationship between *jus cogens* and *jus dispositivum* in Jewish law, see Elon, *op.cit.*, pp. 158-163. The right to stipulate against the rules of monetary law in the *Torah* was developed during the Tanaitic period and accepted by the Amoraim; see M. Ketubot 9.1, Tosefta Qidushin 3.7-8, Ketubot 83b-84a; Rambam, *Yad*, *Ishut* 12.6-9. Within these lines, a commercial *minhag* is a form of community stipulation which annuls conflicting Toraitic prescriptions; see M. Baba Metzia 7.1 and the accompanying *sugya* in the Yerushalmi.

6. The theory, as expressed by Rambam in *Yad, Sh'vitar Asor* 3.3, is that *minhag* is valid when it chooses between permitted ritual options but cannot "permit that which is forbidden" by *halakhah*. See Elon *op. cit.*, p. 738.

7. See the famous incident between Hillel and the B'nai B'teirah, B. Pesahim 66a, as well as B. Berakhot 45a ("*puk hazi mai ama dabar*").

8. M. Avodah Zarah 1.1; Alfasi, *ad loc.*; Rambam, *Yad, Avodat Kokhavim* 9.1 (on Rambam's differing attitudes concerning Islam and Christianity, compare *Maakhalot* Asurot 11.7 with *Avodat Kokhavim* 9.4 in the uncensored texts).

9. R. Asher b. Yehiel, *Hil. HaRosh, Avodan Zarah* 1.1, who summarizes the arguments. See also *Hagahot Maimoniot, Avodat Kokhavim*, 9.1, 2; Tosafot, Avodah Zarah 2a, s.v. *asur*; *Or Zarua, Pisqei Avodah Zarah*, ch. 1, par 95-96.

10. See Haym Soloveitchik, "Religious Law and Change: The Medieval Ashkenazic Example," *Association of Jewish Studies Review*, V. 12, Fall, 1987, pp. 205-221.

11. B. Arakhin 10a and b.

12. Rambam, *Yad Hanukah* 3.5-6, and *Sefer Hamitzvot, shoresh* 1. On the other hand, Nahmanides argues that *Hallel* is a Toraitic commandment on the eighteen days mentioned in Arakhin; see his *hasagot* to *Sefer Hamitzvot, shoresh* 1, where he suggests that *Hallel* is either a *halakhah lemosheh misinai* or is included in the commandment to rejoice on the festivals. See also Rabad, *Hasagot to Yad, Hanukah* 3.6. These arguments, in turn, are rejected by R. Aryeh Lev b. Asher in his *Resp. Sha'agat Aryeh* (Frankfurt a.d. Oder, 1756), #69.

13. B. Ta'anit 28b.

14. B. Pesahim 117a, and Rashbam, B. Pesahim 166b, s.v., *al kol pereq ufereq*, etc. This distinguishes the recitation of *Hallel* on *Rosh Hodesh* from that on the concluding days of *Pesah*. The former is not a festival, while the latter is, and even on *Hol Hamo'ed* unnecessary work is forbidden. See Rambam, quote in R. Nissim Gerondi to Alfasi, *Shabbat*, fol. 11a.

15. *Shibolei Haleqet*, ed Buber, ch. 172, in the name of "*gaonim*." We repeat the final verse of the Psalm in order to add a thirteenth "*haleluyah*" to correspond to the additional *Rosh Hodesh* of leap years.

16. And that *musaf* had to be recited. In Eretz Yisra'el, where the new moon was declared by the *Beit Din Hagadol*, no such reminder was necessary; Meiri, *Beit Habehirah*, *Ta'anit*, 28b.

17. *Halakhot Gedolot*, ed. Warsaw, p. 34d, on the grounds that "whenever less than the whole people of Israel is gathered together, they are called *'yahid.'*"

18. Rav Natronai Gaon, *Otzar Haga'onim*, Ta'anit, #90; Rambam, *Yad, Hanukah* 3.7.

19. *Shulhan Arukh*, Orah Hayim 422.2.

20. Shabbat 23a, where this rule is derived alternately from Deuteronomy 17.11 and from Deuteronomy 32.7. See Rambam (*Yad, Berakhot* 11.3): "The matter is thus, that He has *commanded* us to harken to those (the scholars and judges) who command us to kindle the *Hanukah* lamp, to read the Megillah, and likewise with all other rabbinic ordinances."

21. B. Sukkah 44b.

22. Rashi, B. Sukkah 44a, *s.v. minhag*. See also his responsum in *Siddur Rashi*, ed. Freimann, ch. 540, p. 269: while it is permissible to recite the concluding benediction to the *Hallel*, whose formula does not contain the Hebrew *asher qid'shanu...v'tzivanu*.

23. Exodus 20.7; B. Berakhot 33b; *Yad, Berakhot* 1.15.

24. *Sefer Ha'orah*, ed. Buber, part 2, ch. 59, p. 200; *Isur Veheter,*ed. Ehrenreich, ch. 55, p. 26; *Sefer Hapardes*, ed. Ehrenreich, p. 349; *Teshuvot Rashi*, ed. Elfenbein, #347, p 351; *Mahzor Vitry*, ch. 241, p. 206.

25. *Yad, Hanukah* 3.7. As usual, Rambam follows in the wake of Alfasi, *Shabbat*, fol. 11b.

26. *Halakhot Gedolot*, ed. Hildesheimer, p. 359.

27. B. Berakhot 14a.

28. *Sefer Hayashar*, Heleq Hahidushim, ed. Schlesinger, ch. 537, pp. 319-320. See also Tosafot, Berakhot 14a, *s.v. yamin*; Tosafot, Ta'anit 28b, *s.v. amar*; R. Asher, *Berakhot* 2.5; *Hidushei Ha-Ritba*, Berakhot 14a.

29. See Rambam, *Yad, Tzitzit* 3.9; *Hagahot Maimoniot, ad loc.*, #40, in the name of Rashi; *Shibolei Haleget*, ed. Buber, ch. 295, in the name of R. Isaiah of Trani.

30. *Tur*, Orah Hayim 17. But compare Orah Hayim 589, where he allows women to recite the benediction over the *shofar* and says that it is not a *berakhah levatalah*.

31. The exemption of the blind is quoted in the name of R. Yehudah in B. Baba Kama 87a. That the blind recite benedictions over voluntary acts is derived from B. Kiddushin 31a, where the blind Rav Yosef expresses joy over the fact that he performs *mitzvot* without being commanded to do so. R. Tam: "If he cannot recite *berakhot*, why is he so happy? Do we not learn that 'If one wishes to be a *hasid*, he should fulfill the requirements of *berakhot*?'" (B. Baba Kama 30a). See the following Tosafot passages: B. Berakhot 14a, *s.v. amar*; B. Eruvin 96a, *s.v. dilma*; B. Rosh Hashanah 33a, *s.v. ha*; and R. Asher, Qiddushin 1.48-49.

32. The refutations: 1) blind males are obligated under rabbinic law to observe the commandments, while women are not so obligated; 2) both R. Yohanan and Resh Laqish (B. Berakhot 33a) read Ex. 20.7, as a Toraitic prohibition of the *berakhah levatalah*.

33. B. Qiddushin 31a (*gadol ham'tzuveh v'oseh*, etc.). R. Nissim Gerondi to Alfasi, *Rosh Hashanah*, fol., 9b; Mishnah Berurah, 17, note 4.

34. Tosafot, B. Berakhot 14a, *s.v. amar*.

35. See *Magen Avraham, Orah Hayim* 489, note 1, on women and the counting of the *Omer*. The question of the voluntary acceptance of obligations, forms a major part of the *halakhic* analysis of R. Joel Roth in S. Greenberg, ed., *The Ordination of Women as Rabbis*, New York, 1988, pp 127-187.

36. Isserles in *Shulhan Arukh*, Orah Hayim 17.2 and 422.2.

37. Sometimes, the mere existence of a *minhag* is seen as sufficient justification; see R. Asher, *loc. cit.*: "As we read in the Yerushalmi (Pe'ah 7.5): 'If the *halakhah*

is uncertain, see what practice the people are following.' And the community is already accustomed to saying this benediction."

38. Tosefta, Berakhot 1.1; B. Berakhot 2b.

39. Alfasi, *Berakhot* fol. 1a-b; *Yad, K'ri'at Shema* 1.9.

40. M. Berakhot 1.1.

41. *Otzar Hagaonim, Berakhot #2.* Since the *Shema* is, after all, *d'oraita*, it must be observed strictly. This is not the case with *tefilat aravit*, whose status is not even *derabanan* (B. Berakhot 27b). Rav Hai notes that this procedure makes it impossible to have the *tefilah* follow immediately upon the *ge'ulah* benediction, according to R. Yochanan's prescription (B. Berakhot 4a). Still, if the choice is between following R. Yochanan and reciting the *Shema* at its proper time, the latter course must be chosen. See also Tur, Orah Hayim 235, in the name of Rav Paltoi.

42. For a complete treatment of the issue from a historical as well as *halakhic* viewpoint, see Jacob Katz, "Ma'ariv biz'mano veshelo biz'mano," *Zion*, V. 35, 1970, pp. 35-60.

43. Deuteronomy 6.4-9.

44. Rashi, B. Berakhot 2a; s.v. *ad sof ha'ashmurah harishonah.* The abbreviated q'ri-at *Shema* at bedtime follows the Talmudic dictum (B. Berakhot 60b). Rashi may have received the theory that the *q'ri-at Shema she'al hamitah* is the one which fulfills the commandment from R. Hananel, whose words to this effect are cited in *Sefer HaRaban* (R. Eliezer b. Natan of Mainz, b. ca. 1090), ch. 122 and 171.

45. Tosafot, Berakhot 2a; *s.v. me'eimatai.* See also *Sefer Hayashar, Hiddushim,* ed. Schlesinger, ch. 422. The position of R. Tam is discussed as well in *Or Zaru'a, Hilkhot Q'ri'at Shema* ch. 1; *Mordekhai, Berakhot,* ch. 1; and R. Asher, *Berakhot* 1.1.

46. B. Berakhot 27a.

47. See R. Asher, *loc. cit.*

48. B. Berakhot 2b; Tosefta, Berakhot 1.1.

49. See *Hiddushei HaRashba*, B. Berakhot 2a; R. Asher, *ad loc.*

50. R. Isaiah of Trani, quoted in *Shibolei Haleqet*, ed. Buber, ch. 48. R. Shelomo b. Adret, however, argues that the benedictions surrounding the *Shema* are not *birkot mitzvah* such as the blessings for reading the Torah or the *Megilah* and may therefore be recited at a time earlier than that prescribed for the *k'ri'at Shema* (*Resp. Rashba*, I, #47).

51. This was the practice of R. Avraham Av Beit Din of Provence: say "*amen*" to the *Shema*'s benedictions, recite the *Shema* itself "as one who reads it in the Torah," pray *ma'ariv*, and then say the *Shema* with its benedictions after sundown; *Shibolei Haleqet, loc. cit.* R. Yonah Gerondi, to Alfasi, *Berakhot*, fol. 1a-b, suggests that one recite the *Shema* with its benedictions along with the community but without the intention of fulfilling the *mitzvah*. Then, following sundown but before the evening meal, one repeats the *Shema* without its benedictions and with the requisite intention. (As long as it is sunset, if not sundown, one may properly recite the benediction *ma'ariv aravim*.)

52. R. Asher and *Tur, loc. cit.* A similar *sha'at hadahaq* argument is presented by R. Zerahyah Halevy in *Sefer Hama'or*, Alfasi, *Berakhot*, fol. 1b.

53. *Sefer Ra'abyah*, ed. Aptowitzer, V. 1, ch. 1. See also the words of R. Tam, quoted by Meiri in his *Magen Avot*, ed. Last, pp. 53-54.

54. With the exception of R. Ya'aqov Landau, *Sefer Ha'Agur*, ed. Hershler, ch. 327. See R. Yisra'el Isserlein, *Responsa Terumat Hadeshen*, #1, and R. Moshe Isserles, *Darkei Moshe*, Tur, Orah Hayim 235.

55. B. Gittin 5.8.

56. B. Gittin 59b.

57. This matter is contested in the Yerushalmi (Gittin 5.9), where R. Shimeon b. Yohai regards this as a Toraitic rule and R. Shimeon b. Levi sees it as rabbinic.

58. *Otzar Hagaonim, Gittin*, #s 306-310 (though in the latter quotation, the *gaon* allows a non-priest to receive the honor on Mondays and Thursdays).

59. *Tur*, Orah Hayim 135. See R. Asher, *Gittin* 5.20.

60. *Resp. Rashba*, Vol. I, #119.

61. *Resp. Rivash*, #204.

62. To M. Gittin 5.8.

63. M. Horayot 3.7.

64. *Yad, Tefilah* 12.18.

65. Orah Hayim 135. Karo's close attachment to the *halakhah* of Rambam is evident in his introduction to the *Beit Yosef*, where he calls Rambam "the best-known *halakhic* authority in the world," and in the extent to which he provides commentary on Maimonides' *halakhic* rulings, not only in his *Kesef Mishneh* but also in the *Beit Yosef*. See Isadore Twersky, "*Harav Yosef Karo ba'al HaShulhan Arukh*," *Asufot*, Jerusalem, 1989, V. 3, pp. 245-262; and Mark Washofsky, "The Commentary of R. Nissim b. Reuven Gerondi to the *Halakhot* of Alfsi: A Study in *Halakhic* History," *Hebrew Union College Annual*, Cincinnati, 1989, V. 60, pp. 213-216.

66. *Resp. Maharik, shoresh* 9. Karo opines that the *gaonim* would agree that, though even an ignorant priest is normally called first, should the *kohen* willingly forego this honor a scholar may be called in his stead.

67. With some notable exceptions: see Rabad, quoted in Meiri, *Beit HaBehirah*, Gittin, 59b, and Maharik, *loc. cit.*

68. Yisrael Ta-Shema argues that *minhag Ashkenaz* predated the arrival of the Babylonian Talmud in that region and for centuries preserved its status as equal or superior to the formal *halakhah*. On this point, as well as the tension between the *Tosafists* as representatives of the "new" *halakhah* and the adherents of the older traditions, see his article in *Sidra*, Jerusalem, 187, V. 3, pp. 85-161.

69. Jacob Katz, *Goy shel Shabbat*, Jerusalem, 1984, p. 176.

70. Elon, *op. cit.*, pp. 760ff; Daniel Sperber, *Minhagei Yisra'el*, Jerusalem, 1989, pp. 31-38.

71. Solomon B. Freehof, *Reform Jewish Practice and Its Rabbinic Background*, New York, 1976, V. 1, p. 15. Compare his treatment of prayer in the vernacular (V. 1, pp. 35-40), where there is much rabbinic law on which to rely, to his defense of the late Friday evening service (V. 1, p. 19) and "Sukkah in the Temple" (V. 2, pp. 27-28). Neither of the latter practices is "derived" from rabbinic law, but both are justified, either as *halakhically* unobjectionable or as symbolically useful.

Contributors

Peter Haas - Associate Professor of Religious Studies at Vanderbilt University. He was ordained at HUC-JIR in 1974 and completed a PhD in Judaic Studies at Brown University in 1980. He is the author of numerous articles and books, including the just published *Recovering the Role of Women: Power and Authority in Rabbinic Jewish Society*.

Walter Jacob - Rabbi, Rodef Shalom Congregation, Pittsburgh, President of the Central Conference of American Rabbis, Chairman of the Freehof Institute of Progressive Halakhah. Author and editor of sixteen books including *American Reform Responsa* (1983), and *Contemporary American Reform Responsa* (1987), *Liberal Judaism and Halakhah* (1988), *Questions and Reform Jewish Answers* (1992).

Richard Rheins - Associate Rabbi of Temple Beth El in Chappaqua, New York. He is a member of the Responsa Committee of the Central Conference of American Rabbis. He is married to Rabbi Susan Miller Rheins.

Mark Washofsky - Associate Professor of Rabbinics - Hebrew Union College-Jewish Institute of Religion in Cincinnati. His publications include studies on the development of *halakhic* thought in medieval and modern times. He currently serves as vice-chair of the Responsa committee of the Central Conference of American Rabbis.

Arnold Jacob Wolf - Rabbi, K.A.M. Isaiah Israel Congregation, Chicago. He has published three books and over two hundred articles. He has taught at HUC-JIR in New York, at Yale University and Spertus College in Chicago.

Moshe Zemer - Director of the Freehof Institute of Progressive *Halakhah*; a founder of the Movement for Progressive Judaism in Israel; *Av Bet Din* of the Israel Council of Progressive Rabbis; founding rabbi of Kedem Synagogue in Tel Aviv; author of forthcoming the book, *The Sane Halakhah* (Hebrew).

Bernard M. Zlotowitz - Rabbi and graduate of HUC-JIR, received his doctorate in Septuagint studies from HUC-JIR. He writes the column, "Q & A" for *Reform Judaism*. A senior scholar for the Union of American Hebrew Congregations, author of many books and scholarly and popular articles.